Murder in the Name of Love
The Phil Kennamer Trial

by Jim Freese

ISBN: 978-0-692-63624-4

Table of Contents

Preface

It seems every family has at least one skeleton in its closet. People always hope their deep, dark secret will be forgotten over time, if they avoid talking about it. My grandmother Virginia Wilcox Snedden Hagar had one of those skeletons. This one made national headlines, and my wife and I rediscovered it quite by accident on a short visit to Tulsa.

Grandma had invited us to stay in the guest room of her ranch-style home. As we were unpacking, we noticed a small cardboard box on the closet floor, holding a pile of newspaper articles from 1935. Curiosity got the better of us. We furtively glanced at the clippings, one of which displayed a front-page headline with a picture of an eighteen-year-old Virginia Wilcox. The photo showed her leaving the Pawnee County courthouse after giving testimony in a murder trial.

Murder trial? No one had ever mentioned Grandma's involvement in a murder trial. Granted, it had happened decades ago—but a murder trial? That was a big deal! Why had she testified? Was the victim someone she'd known? Had she known the accused murderer? We were left with many unanswered questions. My wife and I needed to keep an appointment, so we returned the box to the closet floor and left the house, hoping to read the articles later and learn more.

When we returned after a few hours, the box was gone. Grandma had removed it—but why? I didn't dare ask her, because I would incriminate myself for snooping. And I wonder to this day why she had put the cardboard box in *that* closet. Why not in a hallway or her bedroom closet? Had she put it there for me to find?

During the visit, Grandma and I enjoyed our conversations about the Wilcox Oil Company that her father, Homer F. Wilcox, had founded. She spoke of her cattle ranching business, and I learned more about my mom as a young girl. Yet Grandma never mentioned the murder trial. I wanted to ask her, but I felt that if I did, she would relive what I could only imagine was a traumatic time in her life. I just didn't want to broach the topic, that skeleton, especially since I didn't know the scope of her involvement.

This, however, didn't stop me from looking into the murder trial on my own. I needed to learn more. Back at home in Albuquerque, I searched online and found bits and pieces about the trial, including testimony from Grandma's then boyfriend and future husband, Jack Snedden, but nothing definitively stated the identity of the accused murderer.

Then I discovered that it was the murder trial of Phil Kennamer, the teenage son of prominent Tulsan and federal court judge Franklin E. Kennamer. I had never heard this name before— a name and a trial that had faded many decades ago with the passage of time. This information gave me a new direction, but it still didn't answer my questions or reveal how my grandmother was connected.

I looked for the trial transcripts, to no avail. I later read that journalists from across the nation had converged in Pawnee, Oklahoma, to cover the trial, in what would become a national story. What was so sensational about this trial? Who was murdered? Why wasn't the trial held in Tulsa, instead of Pawnee, nearly sixty miles away? Fortunately, the *Tulsa World* and the *Tulsa Tribune* newspapers had covered the trial extensively.

After years of research, I retell the story here, based on the testimonies of a parade of witnesses, filtered through the eyes and ears of reporters from that eleven-day murder trial in February 1935. I reconstructed the developments in chronological order, beginning with the early incidents that shaped young Phil Kennamer, the events leading up to the murder, Phil's motive, and how his life came to a tragic end.

Chapter 1

- Phil's Early Life -

It's 1934 in Tulsa, Oklahoma, the "Oil Capital of the World" during the Great Depression. The discovery of oil in the surrounding countryside makes instant millionaires out of some landowners. People build mansions in exclusive neighborhoods and are living the societal high life. A few notorious criminals, such as Bonnie and Clyde, Machine Gun Kelley, Pretty Boy Floyd, John Dillinger, and Ma Barker, travel through Oklahoma to commit violent crimes: bank robberies, kidnapping, and murder.

With jobs so scarce, ordinary people become desperate and do what they can to stay alive during this time, even breaking the law. These crimes can seem "glamorous" when they make the front page of the daily newspapers, especially to impressionable young teenage boys such as Phil Kennamer, the husky, black-haired, nineteen-year-old son of federal court judge Franklin Kennamer.

In the daily newspapers, the details of the Thanksgiving murder begin to unfold. The crime shocks and captivates Tulsa residents. It's a story about Phil's unrequited love for Virginia Wilcox, the oldest daughter of an oil millionaire, H. F. Wilcox. And Phil will do anything to protect her—including murder.

Who is Phil Kennamer? Why is the crime he commits so sensational?

Philip Kennamer

Philip Millholland Kennamer, born on July 26, 1915, in Madill, Oklahoma, is the youngest of Franklin and Lillie Kennamer's four children. He has been described as a "peculiar" child since birth, with an unusual ability to learn. He has always read books that were extremely advanced for someone his age with a Christian upbringing.

Claude Wright, the son of C. H. Wright, president of Sunray Oil Company of Tulsa and a classmate of Phil's, testifies at Phil's trial that when the family lived in Oklahoma City, five-year-old Phil tied a curtain cord around his neck and jumped out a second-story window in an apparent suicide attempt. The cord didn't break, but the curtain came crashing down. Luckily, Phil landed in a sand pile below.

Phil's family members say that he ran away from home at the age of six, with his blanket and a loaf of bread. He was later found about a mile away from his home, not far from the state capitol in Oklahoma City.

Phil's behavior at such a young age hints that his state of mind has always been somewhat troubled. To understand his psychological makeup and the trajectory of his motives, we should begin to chronicle certain events in his early life.

At the age of fourteen, Phil confides to his older sister, Opal, and a few friends that he wants to run away to Mexico, Cuba, or South America to head a revolution. Phil believes that he will someday rule a country with his superior intellect.

Phil's father, Franklin Elmore Kennamer, a stern United States District Court judge for the northern district of Oklahoma, moves his family to Tulsa in 1930. Soon afterward, he feels that Phil needs a more structured environment, because Phil has trouble staying focused and lacks self-discipline, starting tasks and never seeing them through. So in September of that year, sixteen-year-old Phil is sent to the New Mexico Military Institute in Roswell, New Mexico. Established in 1891 in southeastern New Mexico, NMMI is a four-year progressive college preparatory high school that uses the military model to train and educate its cadets. Uniformed students are taught discipline, respect, and character development in this town of approximately 12,000 to 13,000 people. During the Christmas holidays, the principal informs Judge Kennamer that Phil has run away.

The judge sends federal court clerk H. P. Warfield and his wife's brother to Roswell to locate his son. Fearing that Phil might try to leave the country, the judge alerts postal inspectors around the country to aid in the search. After ten days on the run, Phil is found in Galveston, Texas—dirty, ragged, and broke. After he wrote to a friend to send him clothes, a postal inspector intercepted that package when Phil comes to pick it up. He has been living on a fishing boat. He is quickly sent home, then is later convinced to return to the New Mexico Military Institute.

In October 1931 in Tulsa, seventeen-year-old Phil first meets the very attractive Virginia Wilcox, the fifteen-year-old daughter of oil millionaire Homer F. Wilcox, at a teen social function. Phil is mesmerized by her wavy auburn hair, blue eyes, pretty face, and petite figure. Soon, he has his first date with her, which consists of a progressive dinner that ends with dancing at the home of their mutual friend Jack Snedden. She is Phil's first love, and they go on several more dates, consisting of dinners, movies, and dances.

Virginia soon decides that he isn't her type, however, and that they will be better off as friends. She doesn't have the same feelings for him that he has for her. She has no desire to speak to him and doesn't accept his invitations for any more dates.

Phil has a difficult time accepting her decision and can't let her go. Virginia is that golden ring that's just out of his reach: a class act. He's depressed, as any teenager would be if a beautiful lady refused his advances, but he still hopes that she will come around to dating him again. He continues to send her flowers and candy and write her poetry to express his adoration, but not even his devoted pursuit changes her mind. She's strong-minded and knows what she wants. And it isn't Phil, because, well, he's different. He doesn't behave as the other kids his age do. Phil can be socially awkward, making it uncomfortable for others to be around him. There are times when he behaves as if he is something that he isn't. And at other times, he's an uncontrollable rebel. Yet Phil's love for Virginia never wanes.

Then Franklin and Lillie Kennamer decide to send their troubled son to a school for troubled teens in Durant, Oklahoma, in the late fall of 1931, after a representative from the school convinces them that it will be a good match for Phil.

Phil receives an allowance of $25 a month while at school in Durant, and he uses much of that to purchase flowers, perfume, and candy for Virginia. He expresses his love, his obsession, and his devotion for Virginia to his roommate, Claude Wright, who loans Phil even more money for gifts. Yet Virginia continues to rebuff him. She doesn't want his gifts of affection or any contact with him.

Phil finally convinces himself that he should take the train to Tulsa to have a final date with Virginia . . . then commit suicide to make it look like a hunting accident. He loves her so much that life isn't worth living without Virginia's reciprocated affections. The train trip, that final date, and the suicide never happen, but his obsession continues. Did Phil lose his nerve? Did Claude talk him out of going and committing suicide?

The Kennamer home in Tulsa near 21st and Peoria (2014)

In 1932, Phil and his ill mother travel to San Angelo, Texas, where they live together while she obtains medical treatment. There, she enrolls him in the eleventh grade in a public school, where he remains until the spring of 1933. Phil runs away yet again. This time, he hitchhikes and hops trains to travel to New Orleans. He writes to his mother, saying that he is fine. He makes it as far as Miami, Florida, where his father locates him and wires him money for the return trip home.

Phil runs away from home on numerous other occasions, winding up in California and twice in New York City. Again, without money, Phil is able to travel across the states, relying on hitchhiking or riding the rails, which was popular during the Depression. He has fantasies about traveling the world or joining a revolution or the French Foreign Legion, but he has no passport to leave the country. Many times, he has talked to his family about going to China to start his own revolution and overcome the highly organized Japanese. Phil reads many books on military tactics and is going to use this knowledge to lead his Chinese followers and train them to fight, but his family and a few close friends tell him that his ideas are ridiculous and absurd.

Nineteen-year-old Phil comes back to Tulsa and enrolls at Cascia Hall, a private Catholic school, in 1934. He attends his senior year classes for only a few months before he drops out of school, over the objections of his parents. Did Phil leave school because it wasn't challenging or because school couldn't hold his attention? Whatever his reasons, Phil has bigger aspirations, which don't require a high school diploma. Phil expresses an interest in becoming a writer and doing some traveling. His father encourages him but tells Phil he needs to finish school first. When it becomes apparent that young Phil is not going to complete his schooling, Judge Kennamer helps his son find employment. Phil works as a filling station attendant, before becoming bored and quitting. Shortly after that, he takes another job at the Mid-Continent Petroleum Company for a few weeks, until he realizes his heart isn't in it.

Then Phil and his friend Preston Cochran decide to start an advertising business, and Phil's dad purchases a desk and a typewriter to help them get started. Phil wants to try using his creativity by developing ads for oil companies, including the Wilcox Oil Company, and he imagines making huge sums of money on big accounts. Three to four months later, Phil loses interest in that endeavor, realizing that it takes more inventiveness than he can muster up. Judge Kennamer next calls a friend at the *Daily Oklahoman* to secure a position for Phil to be a cub reporter and makes arrangements to pay Phil's salary out of his own pocket. Phil becomes bored and leaves the job after a few weeks.

Then Phil wants to go to New York, and again Judge Kennamer pulls some strings to secure a position for Phil, working in a lawyer's office as a messenger boy. His family learns that Phil is stirring up trouble by trying to organize two rival Negro gangs in Harlem to come together under his leadership. So his parents, frightened for Phil's safety, feel that it's time for him to come home. Phil's father is frustrated that his son didn't finish school and doesn't maintain a steady job. Not only is Judge Kennamer having to deal with his troubled son, but he must also care for his ill wife and hold down his own job.

Judge Kennamer has a connection in California and makes an introduction for Phil to work at a lawyer's office in Los Angeles, probably as a file clerk. After three to four weeks, Phil becomes restless, quits, and returns to Tulsa. Again, the Kennamer family is disappointed with their youngest son.

Phil is at a complete loss about what he wants to do with his life. Now he turns to the bottle and begins to drink heavily. So much so, that he is often too drunk to come home and crashes at the homes of friends or at the Mayo Hotel with his buddies until the next morning.

Phil Kennamer
(February 1935; Courtesy of the *Tulsa Tribune*)

High Hat Club

Phil becomes a member of the High Hat Club, an exclusive social fraternity whose teenage members are from wealthy and privileged families in Tulsa. The club's objective: *"The promotion of good fellowship among its members, the promotion of good sportsmanship, and the advancement of society in the best interest of humanity."* Meetings are usually held in a living room or a study in a member's upscale home. Any "male person" who is interested can join the club. A candidate has to be sponsored by two members but can be denied membership if he receives two negative votes. Once accepted, he will pay an entrance fee of $3 and a 25-cent fee for each regular meeting, held every Saturday night at a member's home. The club even has a prayer contained in its by-laws:

Most Holy and Gracious Father in Heaven, we who are gathered here in Thy name ask that Thou accompany each of us as we depart from this meeting that we may neither fail nor weaken in the ideals of our creed and Thy love, but become stronger and better each day in the sight of God and man. Amen.

The club's initiation consists of the new member getting drunk and driving 60 mph while turning corners on the city streets without crashing. At the club, Phil can hang out with his friends and be around young ladies who put in their written requests to be paired with one of the club's members for a dance. This allows Phil to join in the social scene with his peers, have a good time, and meet someone of the female persuasion. Although Phil feels welcomed as a member of the High Hat Club, he still doesn't feel complete. He desires more from life.

He desperately loves Virginia Wilcox, but she only wants to be friends. Phil asks Virginia to the High Hat dances many times, but she always politely refuses. He feels sad, depressed, and moody, yet he continues to pursue her. At times, he talks to his friends and his family of committing suicide. He continues to dwell on running away to join a revolution or the French Foreign Legion, a place where misfits, such as him, will be readily accepted. He frequently says he has nothing to live for and feels out of place in the world, but this would change if only Virginia returned his love.

She moves on, however, and dates other young men, both members and non-members of the club, such as Allen Mayo, whose father built the famous Mayo Hotel in downtown Tulsa; Jack Snedden, son of oil millionaire George Snedden; Sidney Born, son of a University of Tulsa professor; and John Newlin. **Jack Snedden**, a "bad boy" who likes to drink, is also a member of the High Hat Club.

Phil and Jack are very close friends and frequent each other's homes. Phil tells Jack many times that he is glad that Jack is dating Virginia regularly. Yet Phil makes it very clear that if he *ever* hears that Jack is mistreating or talking badly about her, Phil will kill him. Is he joking with his best friend or being overly protective? Has Phil finally resolved that Virginia is out of his reach, or is this his way of wooing Virginia by showing her how much he cares?

Chapter 2
1934

- Phil Meets John Gorrell -

Late August

Phil is working at the Frates Insurance Company when he gets a call from his friend and coworker **Preston Cochrane** to come to his office. Preston wants Phil to meet someone. It is the first time Phil and John Gorrell make their acquaintance. **John Franklin Gorrell**, twenty-three, a dental student in Kansas City, was born on July 23, 1913, in Pennsylvania. The son of a prominent and well-known physician in Tulsa, the 6-foot, 2-inch, brown-haired, brown-eyed lad went to grade schools in Tulsa and graduated from the Missouri Military Academy in Mexico, Missouri. John then attended Tulsa University and Oklahoma A&M. He is a licensed government pilot, and he did his training at the Spartan Air School in Tulsa. Now, while enrolled at the Kansas City Western Dental College in Missouri, John is working as a switchboard operator three nights a week at a hotel to defray school expenses. Phil and John will later become co-conspirators in the crime.

Preston Cochrane
Introduced Kennamer to Gorrell

In the meantime, Virginia and her four younger siblings are fishing and swimming at Platte Lake at their summer home near Traverse City, Michigan. Phil misses her terribly, and his feelings for her resurface. He is desperate to know that she is thinking of him. He begs Jack, while at the Kennamer home, to call Virginia in Michigan and ask her if she will please write to Phil.

Phil later writes the following letter to Virginia and asks Jack to mail it:

> *My Dear Virginia,*
> *Jack was over tonight with some information which shocked me. Bear with me in justice to Jack and to yourself while I start from the beginning of what is at least a painful course of events.*
>
> *About three weeks ago, taking advantage of my family's absence, I became rather intoxicated. That is a miracle of understatement because from all accounts I did a more thorough job than at any time heretofore.*

I not only got drunk, I became quite ill, bodily and mentally for some time. I was quite irresponsible in anything I did or said. Jack, who was spending his time nursing me, became quite alarmed. It seems that you were the chief topic of my maudlin ravings. I would apologize for this except for the fact that you would not, and I cannot blame you, to accept it.

Jack conceived the idea that if perhaps he could persuade you to write me a note of the "all-is-forgiven" variety that it might help me to snap to. So while I was passed out, he called you and asked if you to write such a note. I think you know and I know just how absurd that was. Snedden had no way of knowing, however, that it would be impossible for you to consider writing me.

He did what he thought best to assist a friend needing help. There is no finer motive than such friendship.

Jack tells me that he received a letter from you in which you seem angry at him for making the request and doubt the sincerity of his feelings toward you. Permit me to say that it is the most foolish thing in your life. Snedden cares for you more than anyone or anything on earth. What he did, he did with the purest of motives—friendship. A friendship which I do not deserve but hope to keep. I do not know what you said to him but I know that, intentionally or unintentionally, you have deeply hurt the finest person I have ever known and hurt him at a time when he needs the sympathy of those for whom he cares. I know that my feelings are of no interest to you, but I have one piece of information which should interest you. This last "binge" has permanently cured me of drinking. My money ran out and my folks came home almost simultaneously. The illness which followed also did its share in curing me.

The old feeling is dead. Virginia, whatever I said in my delirium came from the liquor and not from me. Towards you now, I feel nothing but admiration, respect and friendship. It has been like that for some time and all I wish in regard to you is friendship. Even that is denied to me, but I wonder—the fact that the old feeling is dead should be a trifle important to you from the fact that it will assure you of absolute freedom of annoyance from me. So long, Virginia. If we meet again, I assure you that it will be casually.

Signed,

K.

Phil tells Jack that if Virginia doesn't write back, he will drink himself to death. Virginia does write, but not to Phil—rather, to Jack. She tells Jack that she won't write to Phil—she just can't bring herself to do it. In September, she returns to Tulsa from Michigan just before the start of her senior year at Monte Cassino School, a private Catholic school for girls.

Wednesday, September 12

Phil Kennamer gets a call at work from his new acquaintance, John Gorrell, to meet him after work at Jewett's Brown Derby Café on South Main Street The café is located in an area clustered with local hangouts, where many students go to eat in what they affectionately call the "Jelly Bean" district. John wants Phil to meet a friend of his, **Ted Bath,** of 1222 South Cheyenne. Ted is in Tulsa vacationing from his work with Sinclair-Prairie Oil Company in Longview, Texas.

Phil is already waiting at the café when John arrives. John immediately brings Phil outside to Ted's car and introduces the two men. He feels that the three of them would work well together and wants to discuss some moneymaking ideas. Ted drives them to the Brown Derby, a beer parlor on South Main Street. The three young men take a rear booth, order some beers, and make small talk.

John looks at Ted and says, "Phil is a close friend, and anything said will be kept in confidence."

The conversation that ensues is about anything *but* how to make an honest dollar.

"I could sure use some extra money," Phil remarks.

"We could, too!" says John.

"I know a place on East 11th Street where they sell beer and sandwiches," says Phil. "On Monday mornings—say, at one or two in the morning—there will be some money. It could be three or four hundred dollars. The three of us should hijack the place and get that money and use it where we could make more money. And you have a Texas license plate," he adds, looking at Ted.

Ted, seemingly leery of the idea, says, "There's probably going to be three or four men there to safeguard any valuables they have. If we try something like that, it could result in bloodshed, and somebody might get killed."

The other two agree and dismiss the idea.

The topic of conversation changes. Ted heads to the bathroom and leaves John and Phil to continue discussing their ideas for making money. Now they come up another idea: have a party, invite lots of friends, and get a girl drunk. But not just any girl—a girl whose family has a lot of money. They will lure the intoxicated female to a bedroom, get her in a comprising position, and take topless or nude photographs of her. She will be so drunk, she won't know who is taking the pictures. Once these pictures are developed, the boys will blackmail her. And no young society girl wants lewd pictures of herself floating around, causing great embarrassment to her and her wealthy family.

John and Phil believe that the victim's family will pay big money to the extortionists to keep those photos from becoming public. It sounds like a great plan that just might work. Now the question is: Who will be the victim?

Ted returns to the booth, and Phil discusses the new idea with him. Phil asks, "Do you know Barbara Boyle?"

"No."

"Leave her name out of it!" John quickly replies. "She's a close friend of the family."

"Do you know Virginia Wilcox?" asks Phil.

"No," says Ted.

"Would it be possible for you to take off from work for a couple of weeks?"

"Not unless there is something of importance or if I'm doing something else."

"I will defray all of your expenses if you make an effort to ingratiate yourself with Virginia Wilcox. Get her into a compromising situation and take some pictures."

Phil makes this suggestion because he wants Virginia to see him as a "hero." Before the nude pictures are made public, Phil plans to explain to Virginia that he learned about them and intervened with the potential blackmailer. Then he'll deliver the photos and the negatives to her, so that she can do what she wishes with them. In Phil's twisted rationale, he believes this scheme will somehow trick Virginia into giving him the love and gratitude he so desperately wants.

"I'm not interested," says Ted.

Mid September

John Gorrell has an idea that he thinks is a lot better than taking pictures of young society girls and blackmailing them. This plan will be more likely to succeed. He shares his new plan with friends Preston Cochrane and Pat Burgess, a reporter for the *Tulsa World* newspaper. John is possibly thinking that by letting Pres and Pat in on the plan, they can get paid for bringing the story to the newspaper and get a cut of the money for aiding in the blackmailing scheme. Neither of the boys wants to participate in such a plan. A few days later, Pres and Pat tell Phil of John Gorrell's plan: to kidnap Virginia Wilcox for ransom.

Wednesday, October 10

Phil has been thinking about what Pres and Pat have told him and is now concerned about it. He tells seventeen-year old Homer Wilcox Jr., Virginia's younger brother, that John Gorrell, whom Homer has never met, plans to kidnap his sister and hold her for ransom. Homer refuses to believe this rumor. He knows how Phil is and about Phil's feelings for his sister. Homer thinks it's never going to happen and it's just another desperate attempt to get his sister's attention. Homer doesn't want to worry his parents and decides not to tell them.

- The Plot and the Confirmation -

Monday, November 19

Phil receives a letter at work from John Gorrell, who is back at dental school in Missouri. The letter asks Phil to come to Kansas City, saying that John has made some connections and he promises they can make plenty of easy money. Phil takes the letter home and puts it on the desk in his bedroom. Later, Phil's father spies the letter and glances over it without Phil's knowledge. Judge Kennamer reads the part about making "easy money." He takes the letter and discards somewhere in his study.

Phil is curious about the "easy money" and wonders whether it's about the plan he heard from Pres and Pat: kidnapping Virginia. If that is the plan, he needs to go to Kansas City to confirm it. The problem is that if he will be gone for a few days to meet John, he needs to tell his parents where he's going so they don't worry that he is running away again. Phil plans to tell them that he's going on a hunting trip with a friend, Jack Land Jr., but needs to collaborate on the story with him, in case Jack Snedden is asked about Phil's whereabouts.

Tuesday, November 20

Phil purchases his round-trip plane ticket to Kansas City for the next day, with the intent of returning the day after that, at 3 p.m. Phil asks Jack Snedden to take him to the airport and pick him up when he returns. Jack takes Phil home to pack a few things. While he's packing, Phil makes a couple of calls: one to his friend Jack Land Jr. to collaborate on the story that the two are going hunting together, to justify to his parents the reason for his leaving town; the second call is to John Gorrell to get his address in Kansas City, because Phil thinks John's letter has been misplaced. John tells Phil that it's 1205 Linwood Avenue at the Linmont Apartments.

He says he will introduce Phil to his gang as "Bob Wilson" to protect his identity.

In the meantime, Jack drives a few blocks home, showers, and then returns to the Kennamer home for the trip to the airport.

"Why are you going to Kansas City?" asks Jack, concerned.

"I'm going to see if Gorrell is going through with the extortion plot. He's got a gang to kidnap Virginia. If he is, I'm going to kill him."

John Gorrell

Jack tries to talk Phil out of it, saying, "There's no need to go to Kansas City. I don't think he's going to go through with it."

Phil is determined to go. Because if the plan is true, he needs to find some way to dismantle it. He needs to protect Virginia.

Wednesday, November 21

Phil Kennamer arrives in Kansas City and checks in as "Mr. Copeland from Chicago" in the new Phillips Hotel, a 20-story, 450-room structure built in 1931 at 12th and Baltimore. He tours the city, returns to the hotel for dinner with drinks, then goes to the Country Day School (now known as Pembroke Hill, a college preparatory school) to visit a former High Hat club member, Fred Koontz. Later he heads off to a local sporting goods store near the apartment building where he will meet with John; at the store, he purchases a pair of rubber gloves and a hunting knife. The knife is a replacement for one that he lost; he decides that it would be a good idea to have something to defend himself with, if the meeting with John takes a turn for the worse.

Phil calls John from a phone booth and arranges to meet him between 12:15 and 12:30 a.m. As he enters the lobby of the apartment building, Phil sees six or eight fellows around the age of twenty to twenty-five, who all appear to be drunk. Then he spots John, who has also been drinking.

"Hi, John."

"Hi, Bob. Everyone, this is Bob Wilson," says John.

Both men chat for a few minutes and move to a quiet corner of the lobby. After talking with Phil, John is beginning to feel a bit uneasy about teaming up with him and may feel a bit intimidated by him as well. Phil has just walked onto John's turf and encounters what he believes to be John's gang. This is an intimidating situation and makes him uncomfortable. If what Pres and Pat told him is true about John's attempt to kidnap Virginia, Phil needs to protect her. He doesn't want to see her harmed, but she needs to see his noble and courageous attributes on his terms. Phil needs to be in control, and John's plan takes that away. Any tactics used must be his own, and no one can interfere with them. This is likely the reason why Phil begins acting aggressively toward John. Nervous, John excuses himself and makes his way across the room to Richard "Dick" Oliver, his roommate.

He tells Dick, "Take a good look at this fellow. If I am killed, Bob Wilson is the one who did it."

John goes back to Phil and says, "Lets go upstairs and talk."

They go into room #502 and close the door. John pulls out his pistol and lays it on the table next to him, for security reasons and as an intimidation factor. John means business, and if Phil makes any wrong moves, John will be ready. They both sit down and get into the details of the plan.

"I've got a red hot proposition," says John.

"I think I know about it. You talked it over with Pres [Cochran] and Pat [Burgess]."

"Yes, but you don't know which proposition it is."

"You mean the Wilcox girl?"

"Yes."

"What have you done on it?" asks Phil.

"Where do you fit in?"

Needing a way to learn more about the plot, Phil says, "Well, I can fit in anywhere."

"Well, I have my plans definitely made," says John.

About that time, the door opens and Everett Gardner, nineteen, walks into the room. Everett is from Enid, Oklahoma, and has a reputation for being a playboy. He dropped out of school in the ninth grade and has not had regular employment in three years. His family made a considerable amount of money from oil found on their farm. Everett has spent much of his time at the Enid airport and taking flying lessons. He owns two planes, one of which he keeps in Enid and the other in Tulsa at the Spartan hanger. Now, he is in Kansas City conspiring with John Gorrell, and he's in on the plan.

Everett Gardner
(courtesy of the *Tulsa Tribune*)

Gardner walks over and just looks at Kennamer, then turns to Gorrell and asks, "Is this fellow alright?"

"Yes, he's alright. I've known him for years," replies Gorrell.

"Do you have plenty of heat?" asks Everett.

"Yes," responds John, reassuringly.

"If you haven't, I have," says Everett, leaving the room.

"What is this?" asks Phil, annoyed at the interruption.

"Those are a couple of fellows like the boys downstairs. They are all working for me."

"What do you mean they are working for you?"

"We've been fooling around with a bunch of petty hijacking. Now, we're ready for some big stuff," says John.

"Like the Wilcox deal?"

"That's it!"

John explains to Phil that Gardner has two planes, a Waco and a Spartan. A few of the boys downstairs are going to Tulsa to lure one of the Wilcox children out into the country, run him or her off the road, and transfer the victim to another car. That car would drive to a field where one of Gardner's planes would be waiting. The plane would fly near Kansas City and land in a field, where another pilot would fly the victim in the second plane to the Fairfax Airport across the river. Either Gorrell or Gardner would then drive the victim to a suburban home, where he or she would be held until the ransom was paid.

"I have the transportation worked out. The one little hitch is the matter of handling the ransom, and I want Preston Cochran and Pat Burgess in Tulsa to handle that. Can you assist them?" he asks Phil.

"Sure," agrees Phil.

"Let's go to Gardner's apartment and talk some more about it with him," says John.

Gardner wasn't there. So Phil suggests that they both go back to his room at the Phillips Hotel to discuss it further.

In the car, Phil now realizes that the plot is not directed specifically at Virginia but at any Wilcox family member. This could mean that his good friend Homer, Virginia's brother, could be the kidnap victim as well. He wants to discourage John from the plot.

In Phil's hotel room, he tells John that after giving it more thought, he doesn't feel good about the plan.

"I don't think this is a feasible plan. There are too many people involved. The idea of using airplanes is complicated. Too many contingencies might arise, and this whole thing is top heavy because of the number of people involved. We should write an extortion note," suggests Phil.

"That would be alright, except for the fact that there would be no reason as to why money should be paid without an actual kidnapping of one of the Wilcoxes," says John, reminding Phil that the original plan of only extortion was not a guarantee. The kidnapping would ensure their success.

"The threat to kidnap would be sufficient to secure a sum somewhat less than the hundred thousand you were originally asking for," said Phil, still trying to influence the situation.

John and Phil discuss the ransom amount over many drinks and finally agree on a lesser amount for the ransom—twenty thousand—and begin to write the extortion note. But they're too drunk to finish it and go to bed with the expectation of having a fresh and sober perspective in the morning.

The next morning, John awakens and wants to finish the note. He shakes Phil awake, grabs the hotel stationary, and composes the ransom note while Phil dresses. John wears the rubber gloves that Phil purchased the day before, so as not to leave any fingerprints on the correspondence. He wraps the finished product in two pieces of paper, addresses it to "H. F. Wilcox," and starts to leave the hotel room to send it airmail.

The extortion note reads:

Sir,
You will secure $20,000 (twenty thousand dollars) in bills of the following amounts — ten thousand in 5-(five) dollar bills, five thousand in $10 (ten) dollar bills, and five thousand in one dollar bills.

You will be given further instructions later on, either by phone or mail by an operator who will identify himself by the symbol at the close of this letter.

Failure to comply with our demands will result in certain and painful "DEATH" for one or more of your children. Keep the said sum in your immediate house, for a moments notice. You must secure the money, not later than Friday noon. You will keep this money on hand, so that if you are notified in two days or two weeks, you will save us lots trouble, and yourself lots of misery.

      Yours in expectation, John Doe.

      Symbol — This is H.F.W. speaking.

      Strict silence, even in your family, must be observed.

The extortion note in John Gorrell's handwriting

"What are you going to do with it, John?"

"I'm going to mail this thing. It's going on a ride back to Tulsa with you on that Braniff [airline]."

Phil sees his opportunity to thwart the plot. "Wait a minute! It's going to ride back to Tulsa with me, but it's going in my pocket. Not in the mail sack!"

By taking the note himself, he now has control of a major element of the plot. If the letter is not mailed, then the plot cannot work, and he has saved Virginia and her family. But if something does happen, he has the proof of the extortion note in John's handwriting.

"Why?" asks John suspiciously.

"Because of the fact that I came to Kansas City and the extortion note being sent from there might constitute too big a coincidence. I will mail it from Tulsa."

"That would perhaps be a better idea," says John, conceding to Phil again. "We need to get you to the airport to catch your plane."

Thursday, November 22

Kansas City Downtown Airport

Phil and John take a cab to the Kansas City Municipal Airport in Kansas City, Missouri, only to learn that the weather is bad, with clouds and rain, too dangerous to pilot a plane. Flights are being canceled, including Phil's. They drive across the Missouri River to the Fairfax Municipal Airport in Kansas to see if Phil will have any better luck catching a flight, but he doesn't. The flights are being canceled there as well. John runs into his acquaintance **Floyd J. Huff**, a fellow pilot and an airplane mechanic from Kansas City, Missouri, and introduces him to Phil.

Floyd Huff has a checkered past. He has been convicted of two felonies. His first arrest was August 21, 1917, for desertion from the U.S. Army during World War I, and he served nine months' hard labor in prison on Alcatraz. After completing his sentence, he was taken to Fort Bliss and sent to France in 1918 to continue the fight with the Seventh Division.

In June 1920, Huff was convicted of two counts of grand larceny in Fresno, California. Huff maintains it was circumstantial evidence, that he was duped into driving a stolen vehicle for a friend. He served his sentence in the county jail for six months. On May 19, 1922, Huff pled guilty in Arizona federal court to transporting and aiding two prostitutes from Kansas City, Kansas, to Phoenix, Arizona, which was a violation of the Mann Act.

Originally passed as the White-Slave Traffic Act in June of 1910 by Congress, the Mann Act prohibited the interstate transport of females for "immoral purposes." Huff was fined $100 and sentenced to nine months in jail.

John Gorrell, who recently obtained his pilot's license, wants to rent a plane and is willing to take a chance on the inclement weather. Mr. Brillhart, the Fairfax Municipal Airport manager, sees that both Phil and John appear to be intoxicated and are certainly not fit to pilot a plane. He tells them something is wrong with the plane and refuses to rent it.

Huff drives them back to the Kansas City Municipal Airport, where the men talk about their dilemma for a few minutes in the airport lobby. Phil now realizes that he's not going to be catching a plane any time soon and decides he should send a couple of telegrams.

The first telegram is to Jack Snedden in Tulsa, who is scheduled to pick up Phil at the Tulsa airport. It reads, "Grounded in Kansas City. Keep your mouth shut," referring to the conversation with Jack and his plan to kill Gorrell.

The second telegram is to Jack T. Land Jr. in Tulsa at the Philtower building. Phil needs to update Land on their "hunting trip alibi" and says that their return home will be later than planned.

With the telegrams sent, an inebriated Phil staggers to the Braniff Airways ticket counter to board a canceled flight. He gives his boarding pass to the attendant, who sees that he is drunk and asks him to put it back in his pocket so he doesn't lose it. The weather is getting worse, and more flights are being canceled. Huff offers to take the men back to his modest home to wait out the weather.

At the Huff home, John makes a call to his buddy Gardner and asks him if there is anything to drink at his apartment. There is, and Huff takes them to the apartment. But Phil is frustrated that the flights are canceled and desperately wants to get home.

"I really need to get back to Tulsa today," says Phil.

"If you want, you can catch a ride with me," says Huff. "I need to go to Blackwell [Oklahoma] anyway for plane parts. So I could take you as far as Bartlesville."

"I would be just as bad off there as I would be here in Kansas City."

"I'll tell you, if you want to buy a little gas and oil, I'll drive you back to Tulsa," Huff says to Phil.

So, Kennamer arranges for Gardner to buy his return ticket to Tulsa for cash. But before they leave, John and Phil spend about twenty minutes playing a friendly game of craps and enjoy more drinks. Even though Phil wins most of John's money, both men are friendly to each other, and John apparently feels no animosity about losing. Whatever undercurrents are going on between the two men stay beneath the surface. One would think that Phil must feel angry at John's planning to kidnap Virginia or her brother. We do know that John, by his earlier comment, is suspicious enough of Phil/"Bob" to tell his friend that if he's murdered, "Bob" should be the number-one suspect. Yet perhaps Phil actually doesn't feel anger at John; he might merely view John as a sort of chess piece in the elaborate game he's playing to win Virginia's heart. This lack of feeling would be the norm if Phil is a sociopath, a diagnosis we cannot make from this distant time in the future, but a lot of his behavior from childhood on does seem to suggest it.

John says to Phil, "I'll be in Tulsa Wednesday evening or Thursday morning. Call me then."

Floyd and Phil leave the apartment and drive downtown to the Missouri Hotel drugstore. Kennamer hops out and returns with a short quart of Black and White Scotch whiskey. It's 4:30 in the afternoon as they head out on Highway 73 toward the towns of Fort Scott and Pittsburg, on the way to Tulsa.

It's a quiet drive. Phil and Floyd say very little, if anything, to each other, while drinking from the same whiskey bottle.

Once they pass through Lewistown, thirty to forty miles south of Kansas City, Phil loosens up and asks, "Do you know why I came up to Kansas City?"

"No. Why?"

"I came to kill Gorrell," says an intoxicated Phil.

It is astounding that in the short time he has known Huff, he tells this stranger his intention to commit murder. Is it the alcohol or Phil's sociopathic personality that explains this admission?

Floyd turns and looks at Phil in disbelief.

"You don't believe me? I'll show you something."

Phil seems to need to show Floyd that he's serious about what he just said. A drunken braggart, he wants to prove he's a tough guy.

Phil reaches up and turns on the car's dome light. He grabs his bag and pulls out the new 8-inch knife in a leather scabbard and the pair of rubber gloves he purchased a day earlier.

"I got the gloves so there'll be no fingerprints."

Then Phil takes out the extortion note that Gorrell wrote that morning. He talks a lot about his love for Virginia Wilcox and how he won't let John go through with the kidnapping and extortion. He curses Gorrell in a drunken haze and says he will do what it takes to protect Virginia. He loves her, and he will see to it that no harm will ever come to her.

Floyd tells him that he should turn the letter over to the police. Phil responds with a resounding "No!" He is going to keep the ransom note to protect her. Maybe he sees it as his ticket to winning her heart.

Phil continues to tell Floyd of his outlandish plan to stop Gorrell.

Phil had intended to rent a plane at the Fairfax Municipal Airport, where Gorrell would take them on "a ride above the clouds." Once in flight, Phil was going to knock John unconscious, then parachute to safety while the plane spun out of control and crashed. Gorrell would be dead, and so, too, would the extortion and kidnapping plot. But because of the bad weather, Phil couldn't execute the plan to rent the plane. Now he has hatched a new plan to kill John Gorrell once he returns to Tulsa.

Phil continues explaining the details of that plan and tells Floyd that he will drive John to a remote area of Tulsa after dark and pretend that he has a flat tire. Once they stop, Phil will let John have it—kill him in cold blood.

The two men make it as far as Pittsburgh and stop at the Thomas Café so Phil can call Doris Rogers, a dental office assistant and Gorrell's fiancé. The two men drive to her home, pick her up, and drive back into town to the Commerce Café. John gave Phil Doris's contact information so that Phil could relay John's message to her. Yet why couldn't John tell her by phone? Perhaps he needed another person to identify "Bob Wilson," just in case something happened, so he asked Phil to take his fiancée to dinner with the gambling winnings. It would seem harmless enough, and Phil wouldn't be alone with her.

They sit in a booth for dinner and drinks. Later, Phil borrows the car to take Doris home and returns to the café. Phil and Floyd rent a room at a hotel and turn in for the evening to make a fresh start for Tulsa in the morning.

Thursday, November 22

The two men arrive in Tulsa about 10:30 a.m. Kennamer asks to be dropped off at the Philtower building at 427 South Boston in downtown Tulsa, for what he says is a meeting with a man. Floyd parks across the street from the building to drop off Phil. Phil's meeting is actually with his friend Jack Land at his office in the Philtower building. Jack takes Phil home and completes the ruse for Phil's parents that they went on a hunting trip. Floyd, who likes to stay in touch with the people he meets, asks for Phil's phone number. Phil writes his name and phone number, 4-0219, on part of the extortion note, tears it off, and hands it to Floyd.

Phil later meets with Jack Snedden, Pres Cochrane, and Sidney Born to show them the extortion note that John Gorrell wrote. Phil plans to reveal to John that the note is still in his possession, in hopes that John will come to his senses and forget about the plot. If John refuses, Phil will turn the ransom note and John over to the authorities.

Wednesday Evening, November 28

Phil calls the Gorrell residence at least three times. He's anxious to talk to John to get an update on the plans to kidnap Virginia. Has John changed his mind? Or does he intend to go through with it? Phil needs to know because he's not the mastermind, and his lack of control unsettles him. Mrs. Gorrell tells the caller that John got in late the night before from Kansas City. Now he has gone to a University of Tulsa football game at

Skelly Stadium (TU vs. Arkansas) and isn't home yet. She will leave a message for John to call Phil.

Alice and John Gorrell, parents of John Gorrell, Jr

- Thanksgiving Murder -

Thursday, November 29

Kennamer Home

Phil comes home after going to a picture show late in the afternoon. He arrives home too late to have Thanksgiving dinner with his parents and gets himself a plate of food. At about 7 p.m. the phone rings. It's John Gorrell, and he wants to meet Phil around 7:30 at the Crawford Drug Store at 19th and Utica.

After eating dinner, Phil approaches his father and asks, "Dad, if I knew of a bunch of blackmailers, kidnappers, and extortionists, don't you think it would be a fine thing if I would catch them?"

Astounded at the question, Franklin turns and says, "Phil, you couldn't get that information or have any knowledge of any such thing as kidnappers and extortionists and blackmailers except from a bunch of gangsters. Those are the only kind of people that engage in that kind of business. That would never do on earth for you to undertake any such thing of that kind because you are liable to get killed and all of the family killed. Furthermore, if you hear of any such thing as that, you come and report it to me, and I will turn it over to the postal authorities and the Department of Justice agents that are employed by the national government to run down that kind of people and that kind of business."

"Well, I thought it would be a good thing to catch them."

"Sure, it would be a good thing, and they ought to be caught, alright. But you are not the one to do the catching."

Thanksgiving Evening, Gorrell Home

John and his friend Charles Bard, nineteen, a student at Oklahoma A&M University, return home from the game and sit down with the Gorrell family for their Thanksgiving dinner. Mrs. Gorrell tells John that Phil has called a few times, wanting to talk. John begins to look very sick and pale. We can only speculate on what has caused this reaction. Perhaps he wonders whether Phil alluded to his mother what they were planning? John may have worried about what to tell his mother if she asks why Phil called so many times. *And for that matter*, John may have thought, *why did he call so many times? Is there a problem with our plans?*

After dinner, John and Charles run upstairs to get ready for their double date with **Eunice Word** and **Hazel Williams**, whom they will pick up around 7:30 at St. John's Hospital at 21st and Utica.

It's about 7 p.m. when John calls Phil to arrange a quick meeting at Crawford's Drug Store, which is across the street from the hospital.

Crawford's Drug Store at about 7:20, Thanksgiving Night

Franklin Kennamer drives Phil to the drugstore at 19th and Utica. He hands Phil fifty cents and instructs him to purchase some cigars, then come back to the car. Phil returns with the cigars but refuses to get in the car for the ride home. He tells his dad he has a meeting with Jack Snedden and promises he will be home early.

Phil returns to the drugstore and sees **Eunice Word**, twenty-one, and **Hazel Williams**, who are waiting for their double dates with John and Charles. It's nearly time to meet up with their dates, so the girls get up to leave, telling the clerk they are returning to the hospital and to have John pick them up there.

John arrives at the store just moments later.

"Your girlfriends have gone over to the hospital," says Phil.

Looking around the store nervously, John grabs Phil by the arm and says, "Step out here for a minute." He quickly escorts Phil outside.

Alone outside the store, John asks, "How's this *thing* coming along?"

"You're too busy now," Phil says. "I can't talk to you. I'll see you tomorrow."

"I'll be through early tonight. I'll have those girls here [at St. John's Hospital] by eleven o'clock. Suppose I see you then."

"Shall I meet you here at the drugstore?"

"No. Meet me at 19th and Utica."

"I will."

The two men part ways. John drives to the hospital, and Phil calls a cab to head to the Owl Tavern.

John and Charles pick up their dates at the hospital, and the four youths drive to Miss Williams's home at 1405 South Baltimore Street. Charles and Hazel dance, while Eunice watches John play with his ammunition, loading and unloading his .22 caliber pistol. John isn't in the mood to dance and is concerned about his meeting later with Phil.

From Hazel's home, Eunice observes John tucking the pistol into the driver's side door pocket, with the handle sticking up for quick access. If anyone else notices it, they don't care because carrying a gun because is commonplace in the '30s. The four youths drive to the Bard home, where they visit for about thirty minutes.

John and Eunice later leave together, without Charles and Hazel, and drive to Cook's Court, a "tourist camp," at 5900 E. 11th Street between Yale and Sheridan around 9:30 to 10 p.m. Tourist camps were popular during the 1930s—places where transients and motorists passing through the city could rent a small cabin for the night. Each cabin had heat in the winter, a fan in the summer, and a bathroom. The cabins would later be known as our present-day motels. After spending about forty-five minutes presumably engaging in sex at the motel, they then drive to a pig stand, or drive-in, for a sandwich and a cup of coffee.

The evening is cold, windy, and rainy, mixed with sleet. John makes it back to St. John's hospital at 10:50, just before Eunice's 11 p.m. curfew. He parks his Ford coach in front of the hospital a few feet from a streetlight, near the drugstore. John exits his car, opens the passenger door for Eunice, and walks her to the front of the hospital, leaving the motor running and the driver's door open. His gun is still in the pocket of the driver's door, in plain sight for anyone to see. This will later prove to be a fatal mistake. He kisses Eunice goodnight, then dashes back to his vehicle to meet Phil at 11 p.m.

St. John's Hospital at 21st and Utica, Tulsa, Oklahoma (circa 1920's)

Early Evening in the Forest Blvd. Neighborhood

Homer Wilcox Jr., seventeen (Virginia's younger brother), and Homer's friend Bill Paden, seventeen, are using Homer's car and his .22 caliber revolver pistol to shoot out streetlights on Forest Boulevard with cousins **Eleanor Vandever**, seventeen, and **Betty Lou Vandever**, sixteen, on their way to see a movie. One of the girls hits the first street light after taking three or four shots. Homer takes out a second light with just one shot. These young kids are from prominent wealthy families and apparently enjoy destroying public property for sport. They're bored and killing time before their movie starts, but this act is still delinquent behavior. After the movie is over, just before 11 p.m., the four youths return to the previous area, where Bill takes a shot at a third light but misses. Homer takes a shot and shatters the streetlight. By coincidence, it's the neighborhood where the body of John Gorrell will be discovered shortly.

(Wilcox later admits in court that they did shoot out the streetlights, and both he and Paden are fined $75. The band of four had no previous knowledge of what would happen later that night and were not involved with the murder.)

Thanksgiving Night: Owl Tavern (Phil's Version)

It's around 8:30 at the Owl Tavern. Phil strolls in and sees Jack Snedden and Randall "Beebe" Morton having something to eat and drink. He sits with them at their table and starts to chat. This is the first time Jack has seen Phil since taking him to the airport ten days earlier.

After eating, Beebe wants Jack to drive the three of them to Morton's home, so he gets his own car, then heads back to the tavern.

Jack, who is dating Virginia Wilcox, asks Phil, "Have you seen Gorrell?"

"I have a date with Gorrell at eleven," answers Phil from the back seat.

"What's going on?" asks Beebe.

Jack briefly tells him about Phil's history with John and his trip to Kansas City to kill John to protect Virginia.

38

"Do you have a gun?" asks Jack, concerned about Phil's safety at the 11 p.m. meeting.

"No. But I have a knife."

"Let me see the knife," says Beebe.

Phil opens his double-breasted coat, produces the knife from the right breast pocket, and hands it to Beebe.

Beebe examines the weapon.

"Okay. Now give it back," demands Phil.

"Not until we get back to the Owl Tavern," says a concerned Beebe, as an excuse to separate Phil from the knife.

Once the young men return to the tavern, Jack goes to the bar and orders drinks, while Phil and Beebe get a booth in the back.

"What are you going to do?" asks Morton.

"I'm going to have a showdown with Gorrell."

"You're going to kill him, aren't you?"

"No."

"I think you are," states an unconvinced Beebe.

"No. You're wrong. I wouldn't get into anything like that."

"If there's going to be any trouble, I'm going to have a hand in it."

Beebe doesn't want John and Phil to be alone together. If there is going to be a fight, Beebe wants to be there to break it up before someone gets hurt.

Says Phil, "No, in the first place there will not be any trouble, and the best way to precipitate trouble would be for you and Snedden to come along."

Phil sees Morton's discarded coat and quietly slips the knife out of the pocket without Beebe noticing. Beebe later finds the knife is missing and realizes that Phil took it back. Beebe refers to their earlier conversation about coming along with Phil for protection when he meets with John. Phil again convinces Beebe that there won't be any trouble but doesn't want to go unarmed when he meets with John.

Beebe, concerned that bringing the knife will cause trouble, insists that Phil give the knife back to him. Phil concedes and hands the knife back to Morton.

"If anything happens, I hope you're comfortable. I am going with bare hands," says Phil jokingly, as he holds up his hands.

Thanksgiving Night: Owl Tavern (Jack's Version)

Jack Snedden and Randall "Beebe" Morton, George Reynolds, Ed Gessler, and a few others are hanging out at the Owl Tavern. It's shortly after 10 p.m. when Phil comes in and calls Snedden to the back of the tavern. He has just told Snedden that he is meeting John at 11 p.m. to kill him with his knife to stop the kidnapping and ransom plot.

Phil takes Jack to a back room and produces the long hunting knife that he purchased in Kansas City.

Beebe takes the knife from Phil.

Jack asks, "Are you going out to kill Gorrell?"

"Yes," says Phil.

Jack becomes upset and talks to Phil in a loud voice. He is astounded they Phil would think of doing such a thing and tries to talk some sense into Phil to abort his murder plot.

"What about your mother and your sisters?" pleads Jack.

But Phil just puts his hands in his pockets, starts whistling, and says, "Calm and collected me."

Jack becomes frustrated at his failed attempts to get through to Phil and walks away from him.

Beebe goes to the back to see what is going on. On hearing of Phil's intent, he sees the knife, takes it, and walks off. Phil follows him and asks him to sit down.

"I want you to see this," Phil says, taking out the ransom note addressed to "H. F. Wilcox, Tulsa, Oklahoma." He hands it to Beebe and asks him to read it.

"Do you see that letter?" asks Phil.

"Yes."

"John Gorrell is the head of a gang in Kansas City. He wrote it in Kansas City and gave to me to mail. But I didn't mail it. John is going to kidnap Virginia Wilcox."

"Is he?" asks Beebe with a quizzical look.

"Yes, and I'm going to stop it. I'm going to kill Johnnie Gorrell tonight."

"With this knife?"

"Yes."

"Are you really?" questions Beebe.

"Yes, sir! I'm terribly in love with Virginia Wilcox, and this is the only thing I can do about it. Johnnie Gorrell intends to kidnap her, and I'm going to protect her if I can."

"Well, Phil, I don't believe you would. But if you really are going to use it, here is your knife." Beebe hands the knife to Phil.

"Well, it's either Gorrell's life or my life, tonight. You will read about it in the morning paper," says Phil.

Randall "Beebe" Morton

Jack Snedden (l) and Beebe Morton (r)

Beebe gets up and walks to the front of the tavern to stand with Jack, and Phil follows. Beebe has second thoughts about giving the knife back to Phil.

"Phil, maybe I had better take that knife. I may want to use it going hunting." And with that, he reaches over and takes the knife from Phil again, putting it in his overcoat pocket.

"Beebe, are you going to send me out with these bare hands to kill Gorrell?" asks Phil with his palms up.

"Yes, if that is the way you want to go, Phil."

Jack and Beebe now believe they have prevented a murder.

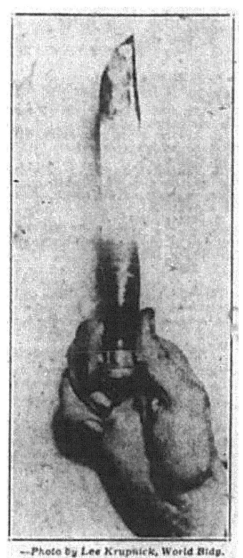

This is the hunting knife, introduced by the state yesterday at Pawnee, as the weapon which Beebe Morton took from Phil Kennamer a short period before Kennamer has admitted he killed John Gorrell, jr. Morton said he got the knife at the Owl tavern.

Phil leaves the tavern and makes his way to the Quaker drugstore next door. It is about 10:45 p.m. when Phil enters and spies **Sidney Born**, nineteen, sitting alone at the counter, having a Coca Cola.

Sidney has always made good grades at Central High School, ranking in the upper fifth in his class when he graduated. He immediately enrolled at the University of Tulsa, dropped out after two semesters, then entered the University of Oklahoma. The instructors at OU described Sidney as nervous and with a high-strung temperament.

Tonight, he has been ice-skating and is drying out after falling many times. **Mary Jo Hafford**, a curb service waitress, is working the evening shift, while eighteen-year-old **Jake Easton** is sitting at a table alone and overhears the conversation between Phil and Sidney. Sidney is the president of the High Hat Club and a good friend of Phil's. There is a great camaraderie among its members, and they will do anything for one another.

"Sidney, I need you to take me someplace."

"Take them," says Sidney, handing the car keys to Phil.

"No. I may be gone a long time, and I wouldn't want the car to sit out. You take me," says Phil.

"All right. Wait until I finish my Coke," says Sidney, with a sigh.

Thanksgiving Evening: The Showdown (Phil's Version)

It's a cold night, and a rain/snow mix is falling from the dreary sky. In Phil's version of the events, he tells Sidney to take him to St. John's Hospital and explains that once they arrive at their destination, he is going to meet John Gorrell, in order to kill him.

Sidney drives to 21st and Utica, turns north to 19th Street, then turns facing west and parks on the north side of the street. John is already parked across the street at 19th and Utica, facing west, where he waits to meet with Phil.

"He is there, alright," says Born.

"Yes, there he is," says Kennamer.

"Be careful."

It's 11:07 p.m. Phil is late. He takes a deep breath, gets out of the car, leaving Sidney, and walks across the street to join John.

He gets into John's car. Sidney drives to the Owl Tavern for a beer, then goes home.

John pulls away from the curb almost immediately, going south on Utica at 35 or 45 mph. The two make some small talk, and Phil asks John about Kansas City.

John wants to get down to business. He turns to Phil and asks, "How's the 'shake'? Did you mail that letter?"

"No," says Phil.

"What's the idea?"

"I never had any intention of mailing the letter." says Phil angrily, to challenge John.

"Why not?" asks John, his voice full of rage.

"There isn't going to be any extortion. If ever at any time you ever consider going through with a proposition of that nature in regard to the Wilcoxes or anyone else, who I count as my friends, I will turn the letter over to the authorities. And if that is not sufficient basis for action, I will kill you," says Phil confidently, in a matter-of-fact tone.

"You will never do anything with that letter," says John.

Realizing he has been double-crossed, John reaches for his .22 caliber pistol in the driver's door pocket and swings it in an upward and then a downward movement, pointing it directly in Phil's face. John pulls the trigger. Click. The gun doesn't fire . . . there was no bullet in that chamber.

Phil, surprised, grabs the gun with his right hand and pushes John's face with his left. In the struggle, the gun discharges, and the bullet strikes John in the head. With control of the gun, Phil fires another bullet into John's head. The Ford coach hits the curb and partly straddles the triangular median at Victor and Forest Boulevard.

John is dead, blood oozing from his head, as he lies slumped under the steering wheel. Phil takes a moment to realize what has just happened. He has killed a man and is stunned, not only by his act but also by the two loud explosions coming from a gun in close quarters. His immediate thought is to erase all evidence of his presence. He looks through the car and finds the gun holster. He wipes the gun clean of all fingerprints, puts it in the holster, and places it on the seat.

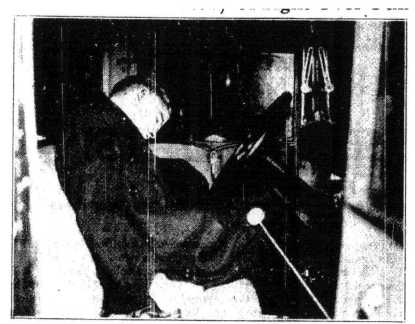

The body of John Gorrell, Jr

Phil leaves John's lifeless body in the car and rapidly walks approximately two miles to the Owl Tavern at 18th and Boston.

It's nearly midnight when Phil arrives. He's cold and wet from the light snow that has been falling. He sees his pal John Newlin at the Tavern and asks him for a ride home to 2135 Terwilliger Boulevard. Phil says nothing of what he has just done and is now in a panic. Then Phil changes his mind. He decides he's not ready to go home quite yet and asks Newlin to drop him off at the Sunset Café so he can get a cup of coffee to warm up and think about what happened.

The Sunset Cafe 110 East 18th Street,
a favorite hangout for Tulsa teens

Robert "Tommy" Thomas, a good buddy of Phil's, is at the café.

"Tommy, I'm in a jam," says Phil, distressed.

"What kind of jam?"

"I just killed John Gorrell."

"In a wreck?" asks Thomas.

"I shot him."

"Why?"

"I had to."

"Where did it happen?"

"Out in Forest Hills."

Thomas doesn't believe him and just laughs. "Take me out and show me the body."

"Tommy, don't laugh, for God's sake! This isn't a joking matter. Just take me home."

"I can't. I have to meet some fellows. We're going to the midnight matinee." Thomas scans the café and sees Tommy Taylor, who is an Oklahoma Military Academy cadet home for the holiday.

"Hey, Tommy!" shouts Thomas. "Will you take Phil home?"

Robert Thomas
Central High School 1933 photo
The first person whom Kennamer tells that he killed Gorrell.

Tommy agrees, and Phil arrives at his home around 12:30 a.m. to find his parents asleep. Phil retires to his bedroom and tries to sleep. All the while, he's wondering how he will tell his parents, particularly his father, a federal court judge, what he did tonight. What will happen to him now?

Midnight at Forest Boulevard and Victor Avenue

Wesley Cunningham, sixteen, is driving down Forest Boulevard just after midnight when spots Gorrell's Ford straddling the triangular median at Forest and Victor near the Titus home. It looks as if the driver has passed out. There is a single frosted-globe electric streetlight on the triangular island, but it isn't bright enough to see too much. Sidney circles around to get a closer look. He uses the spotlight on his car to illuminate the scene, while he stays in the car. He spots a body in the driver's seat slumped over and blood oozing from the head. Wesley immediately drives home and tells his stepfather, Abe Duran, who contacts the police and an ambulance.

Abe and Wesley leave the house to meet the police at Forest and Woodward boulevards to lead them to the scene. The two policemen, Officer **Charles E. Tucker** and Officer Blair, two night watchmen survey the scene. Officer Tucker opens front passenger door and sticks his head in to view the body Seeing the gun, he slides it from the seat and takes the gun out of the holster. He examines it and returns it to the front seat. Officer Blair opens the right rear door to examine the back seat. One of the policemen needs to use the phone, so Wesley takes him to their home, leaving his stepfather, Abe, at the scene of the crime.

The policeman calls **Officer Henry B. Maddux,** who arrives at the scene around 12:30 a.m. His responsibility is to preserve the evidence at crime scenes. Maddux takes a single photograph and removes the gun for evidence. The body is taken to the morgue.

**The trianglar median at Victor Ave and Forest Blvd
where John Gorrell was murdered.**

The trianglar median at Victor Ave and Forest Blvd where John Gorrell was murdered.

Police Investigation

The phone rings in the middle of the night at the Gorrell home. The Tulsa police are calling to awaken Dr. and Mrs. Gorrell to inform them of their son's death. Doctor Gorrell is in shock. He can't be sure whether the surreal news is true or if he's just having a bad dream. He hangs up, returns to the bedroom, and tells his wife of the tragic news. He holds her, while they both sob over the loss of their child. Who could have done such a thing? How did this happen? Dr. Gorrell reluctantly pulls himself away, so he can dress and meet the detectives to identify the body and answer to their questions.

Friday, November 30

Floyd Huff reads about the killing of John Gorrell in a Kansas City newspaper. Recalling the conversation he had with Phil on their drive to Tulsa, he contacts Detective Thomas J. Higgins, the chief of detectives in Kansas City, Missouri. At police headquarters in Kansas City, Floyd hands the detective a small newspaper clipping reporting the death of John Gorrell Jr. in Tulsa.

"Chief, that boy was murdered, and I know who did it! The murderer told me in so many words that he was going to kill Gorrell. He gave me his name and phone number. My life isn't worth a plugged dime. I'm not going to leave here until that man is arrested, until he is locked up tight," says a very nervous Huff.

"Let's get this straight, Huff. Start from the beginning. I'll listen. And if your story is worth anything, you'll get the action you want," asserts the detective.

Huff opens up and tells Detective Higgins the details of his meeting with Phil Kennamer and how Phil was going rent Huff's airplane "to crack Gorrell over the head with a wrench and bail out. That would make it look like an accident. His little plan would have cost me just about eight thousand dollars for a new plane, too."

The story continues with the car ride back to Tulsa: "He kept talking about how he was going to kill Gorrell. Kennamer said that Gorrell is coming to Tulsa next week. 'I'll get him then. I'll drive him out on some lonely road, pretend I have a flat tire. Then, he'll get it!'"

It's a case that is three hundred miles out of his jurisdiction, but Higgins continues to interrogate Huff. The clipping does say that the body "was found in a motor car in a lonely south side park area."

"What was this fellow's name?"

Huff reaches into the vest pocket of his aviator uniform and hands the detective a piece of paper that was torn from the corner of a larger sheet.

"Phil Kennamer. Philtower Building. 4-0219."

"That's the name he gave me," insists Huff. "When I left him in Tulsa the following morning, he gave me that scrap of paper."

"Why did he want to kill Gorrell?"

"Why, he had some rigmarole about a girl he wanted to protect. He showed me a letter he said was an extortion note; that it demanded $20,000 from a man named Wilcox. He explained that the letter threatened the life of Virginia Wilcox, the girl he loved. I didn't read the letter, as it was sealed. Kennamer simply showed me the envelope, which was addressed to Wilcox. Wilcox is a very wealthy oil man, according to what the boy said."

Detective Higgins relays the information to Tulsa police chief Carr by telephone. Both men know that Huff's story needs to be confirmed, but it has to be done very discreetly, so as not to ruin the reputations of a prominent federal court judge and an oil millionaire. Huff demands protection and remains in Detective Higgins's office, for fear of being killed as a potentially dangerous witness.

This morning, Phil rises early. He and his dad drive out to the family farm just a few miles from Chelsea, Oklahoma. Phil is distracted, and guilt weighs heavily on him during the trip to the farm. He wants to tell his father, Franklin, about the incident with John Gorrell but is afraid to, because he's not sure how his dad will react while they're alone. Phil tells his dad that he needs to return to Tulsa to make a $25 payment to the bank. The judge gives him the money.

- December 1934 -

Saturday, December 1

On learning that Gorrell is a dental student in Kansas City, the police call Richard Oliver, Gorrell's roommate, to ask for his help.

"I know who killed Gorrell!" says Oliver. "About two weeks ago, a young man came to Kansas City from Tulsa to see John. John introduced him as 'Bob Wilson' and later said, 'If I am ever killed or wounded, you will know that Bob Wilson did it.'"

Arrangements are made in Kansas City for Richard Oliver's trip to Tulsa for questioning. For his protection, detectives instruct Oliver to get off the train in Claremore, where he will be met by detectives for a personal escort to Tulsa.

This morning Franklin drives Phil to the depot, where he catches the 5:30 train bound for Tulsa. Oliver sees the man introduced to him as "Bob Wilson" get on board in Chelsea. He recalls what John told him in Kansas City. Kennamer sees Oliver and sits near him after entering the coach. Nothing is said, but, Oliver recalls, "I was badly frightened. I could just feel that fellow's eyes boring into me. I got up and moved to the rear of the coach and 'Wilson' moved again."

A frightened Oliver tells the conductor that a suspected murderer is on board, and he's afraid of being ambushed and killed. He pleads for protection, so the conductor locks Oliver in the conductor's personal compartment. When the train arrives in Claremore, Oliver hurriedly gets off the train, where he is met by the detectives. His teeth are chattering so badly, he can hardly speak. Until that train leaves the station, he desperately needs to find a place to hide under the protection of his escorts, where he will not be discovered by "Bob Wilson."

Phil arrives in Tulsa between 6:30 and 7:30 AM and heads to Cascia Hall Preparatory School to take the ransom note to **Father Stephen F. Lanen**, a Catholic priest and an instructor at the private Catholic high school. Although Phil is not Catholic, Father Lanen became a confidant to Phil during the short time the youth spent at Cascia. Phil tells the priest to just hold the letter for him, for fear that he will be killed if the letter is found on him. What Phil doesn't tell the priest is that he murdered John Gorrell.

Phil then makes his way to the office of **A. Flint Moss**, an attorney and a close friend of the family. Phil discusses the incident and asks Mr. Moss to come back with him to the Chelsea farm to tell his father. Moss agrees and they return to the Chelsea farm, arriving about noon. Franklin is devastated and is overcome with sadness once told of the news. How could Phil do such a thing?! What motivated Phil to commit such a heinous crime? Phil explains that it was done in self-defense, but it doesn't mitigate the fact that he has taken a life. He must answer to his crime. Thankfully, Flint Moss is here to help think this through and devise a rational plan to help Phil in a crushingly emotional situation.

It is agreed that Phil, escorted by Flint Moss, will immediately return to Tulsa and surrender to the authorities. Franklin will dress and meet them at the police station. Moss calls Officer Nate Martin in Tulsa and engages in a lengthy conversation to make arrangements before Phil comes to the jail.

It's about 2:30, and Flint Moss and Phil Kennamer arrive at the Tulsa sheriff's office. On the second floor, Moss leans against the railing and beckons to Tulsa County Deputy Sheriff Nathan Martin.

"Nate, I have brought Phil Kennamer down here to surrender for the killing of Gorrell," says Moss.

"Did you have anything to do with shooting Gorrell?" Officer Martin asks Phil.

"Yes. I shot Gorrell," comes the calm, unemotional confession.

Phil is arrested and taken into custody. **Sheriff Charles Price** places Phil in a room formerly occupied by the jail matron, not in a jail cell with the general population. While incarcerated, Phil is allowed many liberties, such as making frequent phone calls, whenever he wishes, to friends. These calls are never censored or supervised. The usual jail rules have been suspended for this son of a federal court judge.

The funeral for John F. Gorrell Jr. takes place at the First Presbyterian Church at 7th and South Boston. It's attended by more than three hundred people, consisting of family and friends. The service begins with music from a mixed quartet, then Dr. C. W. Kerr gives a prayer. He speaks of John's unselfishness, his love of music, and his writing of poems. There is no mention of how John met his death. The thirty-minute service ends with John's favorite song, "Home Sweet Home." The pallbearers are Charles Bard, John Gunn, Jesse Greene, Lon Lyle, Ted Bath, and Jimmie Thomas. He is laid to rest at the Memorial Park Cemetery at 51st and Memorial in Tulsa.

- Media Coverage -

Sunday, December 2

Sidney and his father, Dr. Sidney Born, a geologist and a consulting chemist at the University of Tulsa, report to the Tulsa County attorney's office, where young Sidney describes driving Phil to meet John the night of the murder. Sidney is remorseful and tells reporters, "If I had only known," as tears well up in his eyes. He is in constant fear for his life and asks that the floodlights at his home be left on at night. There are reports that Sidney is getting threatening phone calls and letters that may be coming from Phil, because Phil has access to communication.

Monday, December 4

Phil Kennamer is arraigned this morning in the Common Pleas Court for the murder of John Gorrell on November 29, 1934. The courtroom is crowded with spectators for a preliminary trial that will begin after the arraignment. Phil enters the crowded courtroom wearing a dark gray suit, a gray shirt, and a matching tie, escorted by Deputy Sheriff John Evans. He stands before the judge with attorney A. Flint Moss at his side, with one hand in his pocket, appearing thoroughly at ease and listening to the proceedings. He utters no words as the counselor speaks for him. The attorney tells Judge John Woodward, "We'll waive the reading of the information and enter a plea of not guilty." Phil is remanded to jail without bond after the brief hearing. Franklin Kennamer is not at the arraignment with his son, feeling he must keep a low profile because he is a federal court judge.

Wednesday, December 5

Basil James—a farmer in Wagoner, Oklahoma—was robbed at his home on November 28, the night before Gorrell was murdered. A watch, $85 in cash, and two pistols were taken. While making out his report at the Tulsa police station, he tells the officers that he recognized Phil Kennamer, who was talking to a reporter, as one of the five youths who robbed him at gunpoint.

When confronted, Kennamer denies that he robbed anyone at gunpoint or is part of any gang. The police agree with Phil, because they traced his movements and can account for his whereabouts the night before the murder.

The targets of the kidnapping plot, Virginia and her brother Homer Wilcox Jr., go on an extended vacation with their mother, Olga Wilcox, to escape the publicity.

- The Sidney Born Suicide -

Sunday, December 9

It's shortly after noon, and Sidney Born, nineteen, tells the maid that he's going out and will return in about fifteen or twenty minutes. As he leaves his home at 252 East 27th Street, the maid calls to him that dinner will be ready soon. Sidney's parents are out on a leisurely Sunday drive. Sidney drives to a downtown tire shop to repair a tire. Next, he heads to the Brookside drugstore at 3422 South Peoria and makes a call to the jail to speak with Phil. He talks to jailer A. J. Schultz, who refuses to bring Phil to the phone.

A frustrated Sidney hangs up and says, "Oh, hell!" as overheard by employee Fred Adams and drugstore owner Paul Fowler. No other words are spoken, and Sidney leaves the store.

Sidney Born
1933 Central High School photo
Drove Kennamer to the rendezvous with Gorrell
on Thanksgiving night, 1934

56

Sidney Born's car near Travis Park were Sidney was found shot

Fifteen minutes later, around 1:30, Sidney is found in the small coupe with a single gunshot wound to the head in his father's car on the 2900 block of South Detroit Avenue near Travis Park. The bullet entered the right side of his head and exited through the upper left side of his forehead and through the driver's side window.

The ambulance arrives first at the scene, before the police. William Keenan and Freemont Loper, ambulance attendants, discover that Sidney is still alive. His breathing is labored, and fresh blood is streaming down his right cheek. They open the driver's door to tend to the young man, and as they lift him from the vehicle, a .32 caliber gun covered in blood falls to the pavement. Loper picks up the gun with a handkerchief, inadvertently wipes away any fingerprints, and replaces it in the driver's seat. The police arrive minutes later to begin their detailed investigation, just as the ambulance pulls away, headed for Morningside Hospital. Sidney never regains consciousness. He dies five hours later, making this the second suspicious death of a young man in ten days, just blocks from each other. Both men were from prominent Tulsa families, and both deaths are somehow related to Phil Kennamer.

Professor Born says the .32 caliber revolver used in Sidney's death is his but was hidden at the family home. He wasn't aware that Sidney knew where it was concealed.

The death of Sidney Born sends shock waves of fear throughout Tulsa. Sidney had spoken to the police days earlier and had given them whatever information he had about Phil's involvement in John's murder. Now he's dead, and a full-scale investigation is underway. His suspicious death is being treated as a murder. Did a member of Gorrell's gang murder Sidney? Was Sidney's death revenge for his driving Phil to the meeting with John? Or was a member of Phil's gang seeking retribution for Sidney's talking to police? Or maybe Sidney couldn't handle the fact that he unknowingly aided Phil in killing John, so he killed himself? Sidney's death shrouds the city in a deep mystery concerning the Gorrell murder case and the involvement of both Phil and Sidney.

Professor Sidney Born, Sidney's father, a prominent engineer and a member of the University of Tulsa, makes a statement to the Tulsa newspapers about his son's apparent suicide: "My son would never have done such a thing. He was too level headed." He hires a well-known detective agency to investigate whether it was murder or suicide.

During religious services at the jail, Phil is told of Sidney's death. He becomes very upset and screams that Born was his best friend. Phil is escorted back to his cell, and once he becomes calm, he calls for his attorney. Phil claims that Born was murdered by Gorrell's gang, but the police can't prove it and declare it suicide.

"Born was murdered. I know of three persons who would have reason to do it and who are capable of it. Born could have helped my defense, and he may have talked too much of what he knew of other things," says Phil, from his jail cell to a newspaper reporter.

Tuesday, December 10

Homer Wilcox Jr. and his father report to the Tulsa police department, where the younger Wilcox is arrested for "malicious mischief" and for questioning in the deaths of John Gorrell and Sidney Born. Homer admits to shooting out streetlights in the area where Gorrell's body was found. He bails out of jail for $500. Father and son exit the police station and make no comments to the media.

Ted Bath tells the authorities that he is leaving town because he fears "Kennamer's gang" will try to kill him. Clearly afraid for his safety, he won't tell authorities who the members of Phil's gang are.

"Kennamer's gang is still out of jail and will do everything they can to keep the fellows from testifying. I'm leaving Tulsa for good. The only reason I haven't received threats to keep my mouth shut is because those fellows could not reach me. Plenty of the fellows who told police what they knew about Kennamer and his gang have been warned. So I'm getting out while I'm able. There are too many dark streets and alleys where a shot could seal your lips for good."

The funeral for Sidney Born takes place at 2 PM at the Martin Fleming Funeral Home. The Reverend F. H. Eckel Jr., rector of the Trinity Episcopal Church, which the Born family attends, performs the services. The pallbearers, Billy McBirney, Claude Wright, Robert Thomas, Jerry Bates, Roy Mead Jr., and Jack McKay, are all friends of Sidney's.

The mayor of Tulsa, T. A. Penny, tells the local media that this situation is the fault of the parents, after he learns that the children of these prominent parents get a liberal allowance each week and spend most of it drinking and gambling at the Idle Hour Inn nightclub owned by Wade Thomas. Thomas has been held in custody and questioned since the murder of Gorrell.

Wade Thomas, owner of the Idle Hour Inn

Says the mayor, "The parents of these children involved in this terrible scandal should carry the biggest share of the blame. They have been so busy making money, they have neglected the raising of their children."

Dr. Truman A. Penney
Tulsa mayor from 1934 to 1940

Since the death of Sidney Born, three young witnesses for the Gorrell case—Homer Wilcox Jr., Jack Snedden, and Pres Cochrane—have suddenly gone missing, and their relatives claim they don't know where they are. After talking with Phil in jail, assistant prosecuting attorney Dixie Gilmer says, "I had a talk with Philip Kennamer, and he told me to keep a close watch on these guys. He seemed to be afraid they are in danger, so I've ordered guards for them." Because the youths may be asked to testify in the trial, and their lives may be in danger, Gilmer's guards watch and protect Jack Snedden, seventeen; Pres Cochrane, twenty-one; and Homer Wilcox, seventeen.

Charles Bard, a nineteen-year-old student at Oklahoma A&M in Stillwater, who was double dating with Gorrell the night of his murder, has withdrawn from classes and is asking county authorities for protection.

Holly Anderson, the county prosecutor in the case, has contended since the onset of the Gorrell murder that a gang of well-to-do, thrill-seeking youths has been operating in Tulsa. He says that these youths have been running narcotics between Tulsa and Kansas City, and they go unnoticed because of their social standing. The police confirm that blackmail, extortion, and kidnapping plots have been substantiated in the "fertile minds of youths."

Virginia Wilcox
(courtesy of the *Tulsa Tribune*, February 1935)

Homer Wilcox, Jr.
Virginia's younger brother
(courtesy of The Gateway to Oklahoma History)

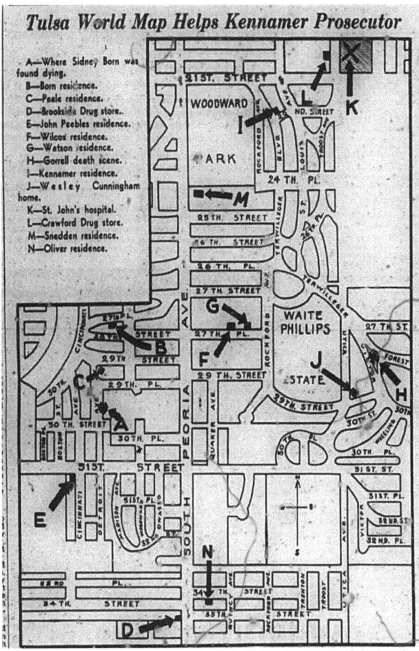

Tulsa World Map Helps Kennamer Prosecutor

A—Where Sidney Born was found dying.
B—Born residence.
C—Peale residence.
D—Brookside Drug store.
E—John Peebles residence.
F—Wilcox residence.
G—Watson residence.
H—Gorrell death scene.
I—Kennamer residence.
J—Wesley Cunningham home.
K—St. John's hospital.
L—Crawford Drug store.
M—Snedden residence.
N—Oliver residence.

A map of the Forest Hills Neighborhood in Tulsa that was used during the trial

Wednesday, December 11

Dr. Sidney Born starts his own investigation into the death of his son. He hires detectives "to get the facts regardless of what they might mean to me or of where they might lead."

Homer Wilcox Jr. appears in Municipal Court before Judge A. A. Hatch today and pleads guilty to malicious mischief for shooting out streetlights in Forest Hills, where the body of John Gorrell was found. Judge Hatch points out that he believes the prank was a coincidence and there is no connection to the murder.

The seventy-year-old judge gives Homer a stern lecture, telling him that he hopes "your father will take the amount of this fine from your Christmas allowance. You have too many pleasures and conveniences. You should have suffered a few privations and hardships. It would have helped you to think about the rules of society." The judge fines Homer $75, which is paid by his father's attorney, Shell S. Bassett.

Homer's friend Bill Padon is arrested and charged with the same crime and is held under $500 bond for his trial tomorrow.

- The Coded Notes -

Monday, December 17

Phil attends his preliminary hearing, and the court orders him to be held for trial in District Court.

The preparations for the trial begin. Now that Sidney is dead, the statements that he made during the Gorrell investigation will be inadmissible in court. The one person who could exonerate Phil has been silenced. Since Gorrell told Pres and Pat of his plot to kidnap Virginia, Phil wants to make sure they take the stand in his defense. Phil plans to write cryptic notes in code that only he and Pres will understand.

This strange arrangement involves Lee Krupnick, a *Tulsa World* photographer, who acts as the intermediary to smuggle the notes in and out of jail. Lee informs Sheriff Price of Phil's clandestine plan and asks his deputies to stand guard to ensure that the two are not interrupted while passing the notes. There are rumors leaked by the press that Phil had others aiding him in

Gorrell's murder and that Sidney's death was not a suicide. It's Lee's hope that he can decipher the coded messages, cash in on the stories to the *Tulsa World*, and give the sheriff more information about the two deaths.

Thursday, December 20

Lee has already taken a few photos of Phil but wants to see if he can get better headshots. He contacts Phil about getting those close-ups of him at the county jail. After Lee takes several photos; Phil asks him to bring the prints back so he can pick the one he likes for the *Tulsa World*. Phil also asks Lee if he will bring a photo of Homer Wilcox Jr.

Lee says he will but checks with the sheriff's office to see whether it's all right. The sheriff's office grants permission, but they put a pinhole in the Wilcox photo so it can be identified, in case Phil tampers with it.

Lee returns with Wilcox's picture and talks to Phil at length about the case. Phil mentions several times that he believes Sidney was murdered by a Tulsa youth. When Lee asked why, Phil jumps at Lee, which scares him. Phil takes a pencil out of Lee's pocket and walks to the corner of the room.

"You stay over there, Lee," says Phil. "Leave me alone for a few minutes."

A short while later, Phil approaches Lee and hands him a folded piece of paper. "Give that to Cochrane. Tell him I said 3-2. Don't forget to tell him I said 3-2."

Lee leaves the jail cell, opens the note, and sees that it's written in code. He takes the note to the sheriff's office, makes a copy, and successfully deciphers the message. The note reads: "Can we depend on Pat?"

Coded note number 1
(*Tulsa World*, **February 10, 1935, pg. 1**)

The reference is to Pat Burgess, a reporter at the *Tulsa World*. Once this note is passed and decrypted, a midnight conference convenes at the Mayo Hotel with Sheriff Price, County Attorney Holley Anderson, Chief Criminal Deputy John Evans, Deputy Tony Benson, and Lee Krupnick. Is there something else they don't know about? Has another crime occurred that involves Phil? The county officials discuss and approve the process that will allow Lee to continue to smuggle future cryptic notes into and out of the jail. Attorney General J. Berry King approves the arrangement. Could these notes be the tip of the iceberg to uncover a bigger plot?

The plan will work as follows: When Lee comes to the jail to visit Phil, Sheriff Price will post himself at the elevator door, where he will be able to see anyone coming up to visit Phil. The sheriff will have John Evans ring the buzzer in the jail. Tony Benson will be upstairs ready to receive the signal that a visitor for Phil is coming. Benson will knock on the cell door to tell Kennamer that he has a visitor. This will be Lee's signal to vacate the cell.

On one occasion, Lee sees rats scampering across the jail floor at Phil's feet and comments, "Gee, look at those rats."

"Yes. I see," says Phil. Then, after a pause, he says, "And there are a lot more rats outside, Lee."

Pres doesn't receive the original note right away, because he is out of town. When he returns and receives the note, Pres cryptically responds: "Yes. Is afraid he will get mixed in this. Burn this."

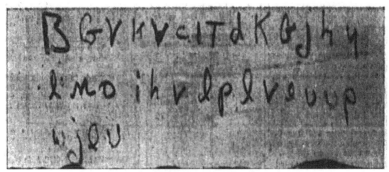

Coded note number 2
(*Tulsa World*, February 10, 1935, pg. 1)

Lee talks Pres into writing another note to Phil. The note is passed to Phil but not before it is deciphered.

The third note from Pres to Phil reads: "I'm for you you know that. Would have been up to see you but Moss says not now. Law thinks I know something and are laying for me. (GJE)." (*Tulsa World*, February 10, 1935, pg. 1)

Lee wants Pres to sign the note, but Pres is reluctant to identify himself and instead signs the note "GJE." When Lee asks what it means, Pres says, "Only two men living—Phil and myself —know what that means." Pres reluctantly divulges that the "GJE" is a coded signature for "Douglas Montgomery Blair," a name that Pres used when he and Phil traveled to hotels together. Phil used the name "Richard Barnard."

Friday, December 21

Phil feels that passing notes is getting too risky and conveys this to Lee. Lee doesn't want the flow of information to stop. So he discards the note from Phil and types another one of his own in the same code (note number 4) and makes additional comments about Pat Burgess, at the direction of his employer, the *Tulsa World.*

Note number 4 from Phil to Pres, which was forged by Lee.

It reads: "Stay away from reporters. Lee is ok. Other birds are swine. Give me more facts. Don't worry I will burn your answer. I am doubtful about Pat. He might talk. Give me actual low-down. I have lots to confide in you. Tell me all. Be sure and typewrite. Don't ever write. We sure can depend on Lee. A real pal. What's doing? You know what I mean. Hurry with your answer. Keep your chin up fellow." (*Tulsa World*, February 10, 1935, pg. 12)

Phil reads this message and instructs Lee what to write in his response. Yet Lee is concerned that Pres will see that the note is not in Phil's writing, will get suspicious, and will stop writing the notes. Nevertheless, Lee types the coded note.

Pres receives the typewritten note and, as expected, gets suspicious. He thinks it's odd that Phil has access to a typewriter.

Lee truthfully explains that Phil has the use of one because he's staying in the matron's quarters at the jail.

Saturday, December 22

Lee and Pres meet at the Modernistic Café at 118 West 4th Street to exchange note number 5. Pres passes Lee a match carton containing the message under the table.

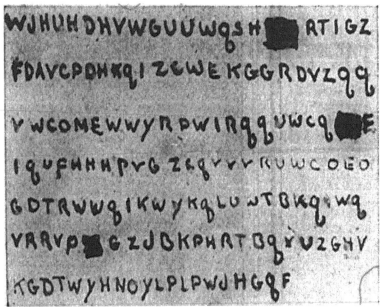

Note number 5 from Pres to Phil

It reads: "These better stop for a few days. Am being watched. Pat won't talk. But won't go on stand for defense. Wants to stay clear out of it. Who is trying to spot me? Why I am for you sweetheart. We'll win in the end."

This note in Pres's handwriting never reaches Phil. Lee substitutes Pres's note for another note, which deletes "These better stop for a few days. Am being watched." So the notes will continue to be exchanged (*Tulsa World*, February 10, 1935, pg. 12).

Sunday, December 23

Lee goes to the jail and finds Phil sleeping. He rouses him awake.

"Lee, bring me my trousers."

Lee hands him his pants, and Phil takes a typewritten note from the pocket. He hands the note to Lee and says, "Tell Cochrane 3-5," implying a change in the code.

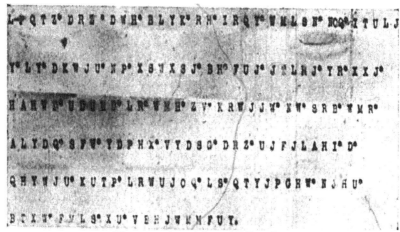

Note number 6 from Phil to Pres

It reads: "I know you are with me. Don't think I'll forget it. After I am sprung we are going to sue every paper in the United States. Forget it now though. Vital Pat takes stand. You received a letter from Gorrell in November. Keep your chin up sweetheart." (*Tulsa World*, February 10, 1935, pg. 12)

Lee gives the message to Pres and arranges to meet him the next day, to obtain the note Pres will write in reply.

\
Monday, December 24

Pres and Lee meet in the evening at the Modernistic Café to pass another typewritten note.

Note number 7 from Pres to Phil

Lee takes Pres's handwritten note and gives it to the county authorities but types the same message to give to Phil (note number 7). It reads: "Merry Christmas. Don't understand about Snedden except that he tried to frame me. Same one, I know who. My chin's up. How's yours?" (*Tulsa World*, February 10, 1935, pg. 12).

Lee takes this message to Phil, who tells Lee, "Don't come up tomorrow. That's Christmas. All my folks will be here. Wait until after Christmas."

Wednesday, December 26

Lee goes to the jail for another visit with Phil. He wants to see if he can find out more about the reference to the Gorrell letter that Phil mentioned in a previous note to Pres. Lee perches on the bed, and Phil sits quietly in the rocker with his head in his hands.

After several moments of silence, he looks up at Lee and says, "Listen, you tell him not to worry about that Gorrell letter, that I will say that he lost it. Be sure and tell him Pat must take the stand."

Lee wants him to put it in writing, and Phil just hands him the handwritten, uncoded note (note number 8): "Skip matter of epistle [Gorrell letter]. Find out if Pat hasn't been 'contacted' by some one from the gang, which is out to get me—keep your chin up and don't worry. K."

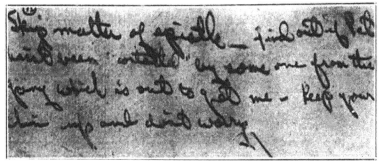

Phil's uncoded note number 8 to Pres

Lee doesn't deliver this version of the note but writes another cryptic version to give to Pres (note number 9): "Don't worry about Gorrell letter. I will say you lost it. You and Pat be sure to take the stand."

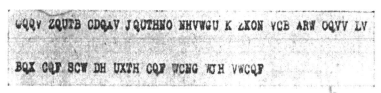

Note number 9, the note that Lee substitutes to Pres

This is the last note that is exchanged, because Phil somehow finds out that the notes are going through the sheriff's office (*Tulsa World*, February 10, 1935, pg. 12).

Note: Pres Cochrane developed this code as a student in Vienna, Austria, while working for the editorial department of the *Tulsa World*. A revolt in Austria was imminent, and Pres feared that if the government intercepted his reports on the conditions in Vienna, he might be imprisoned. Phil and Pres referred to the code as "the 3-2."

To code a message using the "3-2" method and the alphabet, take the first letter and move 3 letters to the right; then 2 letters to the right for the second letter; the third letter would be coded by moving 3 letters to the right; the fourth letter by moving 2 letters to the right; and so on. For example, "Phil" would be coded as "sjln." To decode "sjln," simply move 3 letters to the left from "s," then 2 letters from the left of "j," 3 letters to the left of "l," and then 2 letters to the left of "n."

Chapter 3
1935

- Coded Notes Revealed to the Press -

Wednesday, January 2

County authorities reveal the interception of coded messages between Phil Kennamer and Pres Cochrane. Holly Anderson reveals that he requested a conference with Pres to discuss the passing of the coded notes. Anderson asks that he speak only to Cochrane, without his attorney, N. A. Gibson, being present. Cochrane complies, and afterward, Anderson is satisfied with the meeting. Pres asks that the coded notes be returned to him, but Anderson refuses, saying the notes contain nothing of importance.

Friday, January 4

Phil is formally arraigned in district court with fifty-nine other defendants awaiting trial. The court session was scheduled for 1:30 PM. but since Judge Thurman is late in leaving Pawnee, the session is rescheduled for 3 PM. Phil's plea of not guilty takes all but sixty seconds.

Wednesday, January 9

Sheriff Garland Marrs, the new sheriff since taking over the office on Monday, January 7, has changed the jail rules for Kennamer. Phil is refused permission to see his friends; visitors are limited to his attorneys and members of his family. He is not allowed to leave his room, where he eats all of his meals, and he has no privileges. All furniture is removed from his room, except a dresser and a bed.

- Trial Preparation -

Saturday, January 12

The alienists (an archaic term for psychiatrists who assess the competence of a defendant in a court of law) who are hired by the defense then interview Phil in jail for their examination. They report that Phil is "legally insane."

Sunday, January 13

Holly Anderson, County Attorney, charges that the state's witnesses are being tampered with. Floyd Huff has been contacted in Kansas City by a Tulsa attorney who is not connected with the prosecution, regarding Huff's testimony about the death threat and the plot that Phil made to take John Gorrell's life. Anderson says that he has proof that "approaches" have been made to two other state witnesses.

"We are not at this time going to make a full public disclosure of these 'tamperings' movements. We are not mistaken, and neither is Huff. We are positive that overtures have been made to Huff, who promptly refused to have anything to do with this lawyer," says Anderson. "We have not yet learned the reactions of the other two witnesses. We are not indulging in any guesswork and won't stand for any more nonsense of this sort. If this doesn't stop immediately, someone is going to be arrested and prosecuted."

Defense Attorney Flint Moss agrees with Anderson that if there has been any witness tampering, he challenges Anderson to arrest and prosecute that person. Anderson says that he and Attorney King plan to interrogate every state witness in the next two weeks to see if anyone has made an effort to tamper with their testimony.

Monday, January 14

Ernest W. Marland begins his term as governor of Oklahoma.

Monday, January 21

Phil's defense team believes that Phil cannot get a fair trial in Tulsa and asks for a change of venue for a number of reasons: the widespread publicity in Tulsa—namely, the investigation in the Forrest Hills neighborhood and the prominence of the families involved—plus the rumors surrounding the case. They ask that the trial be moved to Pawnee.

Wednesday, January 23

Judge Thurman Hurst, who will preside over the case, grants the change of venue, so as not to jeopardize the defendant's rights.

The prosecution has no problem with the change of venue, because it doesn't need to establish a motive for the murder but rather merely show that Phil did kill Gorrell and had threatened to kill him on numerous occasions.

Wednesday, January 30

The jury panel is drawn at Pawnee, and the state subpoenas forty witnesses.

- The Trial Begins -

Friday, February 1

The defense subpoenas its witnesses.

Telephone and telegraph companies are busy at Pawnee's new courthouse
threading a network of wires for the Phil Kennamer murder trial
(courtesy of The Gateway to Oklahoma History)

Friday, February 8

As of today, subpoenas have gone out to 107 witnesses to testify next week in Pawnee County District Court for the case: 59 for the state and 67 for the defense. Nineteen of those will testify for both the state and the defense and include:

Betty Watson; John Arnold, tavern operator; Preston Cochrane; John Newlin; Robert Garvey; Pat Burgess; Tom Taylor; Thomas Cox; Randal Morton, Nathan Martin; Wesley Cunningham; Jack Snedden; Ed Gessler; Eunice Word; Dick Oliver; Detective H. B. Maddux; Jake Easton Jr.; Virginia Wilcox; and her brother Homer Wilcox Jr.

The presiding judge, Thurman Hurst, was born on April 28, 1889, in Cassville, Missouri. He moved with his parents to Oklahoma Territory in 1892, where his father made the run in the Cherokee Strip in 1893. The family farm is five miles north of Pawnee. Judge Hurst was schooled in Pawnee. After graduation, he went to the University of Oklahoma Law School in 1909. He received his law degree in 1911 and returned to Pawnee, where he served as an assistant county attorney for Redmond Cole for a short time.

The judge later moved to Weleetka and began private practice for two years. In 1914, he was elected Okfuskee County Attorney and again in 1916. He returned to Pawnee in 1918 and practiced until 1930, where he was elected as District Judge of Pawnee and Tulsa District counties. During the state bar exam, the State Supreme Court ruled that members of his class were automatically admitted to the bar when they received their law degrees. Hurst and other members of his class walked out in the middle of the exam, which ended their examination. Judge Hurst is married with three children.

Judge Thurman Hurst will preside over the trial

Saturday, February 9

Phil learns today from his defense team that he will be taking the stand to tell his story to the jury. His defense attorneys, after weeks of deliberation, announce their decision to the press. Rumors begin to fly on whether Phil plans to rely more heavily on his self-defense plea.

Edna Harmon, of 1312 South Quaker, has contacted Doctor and Mrs. Gorrell to say that she has some information that may be helpful to their case against Phil Kennamer. After notifying county attorney Holly Anderson, the Gorrells take her to the Tulsa County attorney's office, where they hurry Edna into a private office with a stenographer to write down her story. After the meeting, Anderson issues a subpoena for her to testify at the murder trial that begins Monday morning.

"Only four people know what she will tell . . . she, Doctor Gorrell, Tom Wallace, assistant county attorney, and myself," Anderson tells reporters. "If anything about her testimony gets out, I'll know where it came from. The state is entitled to one secret, and she's my secret."

When another reporter asks Anderson if he considers her a vital state witness, his response is "What do think I'm so secretive about?" He declines to say what Edna Harmon's testimony might be or how it would change the course of the state's case but does say that "she has information of importance to the state."

Sunday, February 10

The city of Pawnee, population 2,500, comes alive with anticipation of Phil Kennamer's arrival. Hundreds of people congregate on the courthouse grounds, including "attractively attired women, business men, blanket Indians, bucks and squaws, cowboys seated on horses, uniformed boy scouts, a neighborhood football team and many others," to view the prisoner whose trial will begin tomorrow. Vendors of peanuts and sodas have set up shop on the grounds to sell their goods.

The town's only two hotels, the Pawnee and the Graham, are filling up fast, as hundreds of officials, witnesses, principals, and visitors arrive in buses, trains, and automobiles. Boardinghouses and private homes are renting rooms, and businesses hang out their welcome signs, offering their hospitality to visitors.

Special desks are brought and accommodations are made in the courthouse for the sixty-two reporters who have descended on the small town. Telephone and teletype facilities and a photo studio have been installed.

Phil arrives at the Pawnee Courthouse at 3 PM, wearing a blue suit, a gray shirt, and a blue tie, with Tulsa deputy sheriffs John Evans and E. E. Benson. They surrender him to Sheriff C. M. Burkdoll, Under Sheriff E. R. Ferguson, and Deputy Sheriff J. H. Wilkerson, in the office of the Pawnee District Court clerk Nora Harshbarger, where the transfer papers are signed. Many photographers attempt to take Phil's picture, but Phil curses at them and the Tulsa newspaper reporters. One of those reporters is Lee Krupnick, who slips in with seven other photographers.

The Pawnee County Court, circa 1930s

The Pawnee County Courthouse, 2014

Phil sees Lee in the group of photographers, turns to Sheriff Burkdoll, and asks, "Do I have to stay in the same room with that [expletives] rat, Krupnick?"

"What's the matter with you, Phil?" asks Lee. "Don't you know when a friend is trying to help you?"

"Aw, you rat!" responds Phil and curses again at Lee.

"What happened to all your friends, Phil?" asks Lee. "None of them came up to the jail to see you. You're just trying to be a hero and take the rap for the other fellows."

"I guess I know how I killed him," retorts Phil.

"I mean that extortion note," counters Lee.

"Well, that's my affair. And I want it understood that anybody can have pictures of me, except that rat Krupnick."

"Why do you want to act like that, Phil? You were a newspaper man once."

"I never was a newspaper man," says Phil. "I was a cub reporter once, but I got out of that business as soon as I found out what kind of people I had to associate with."

Lee tries to get a photo of Phil, but Phil keeps turning away. After thirty minutes, Lee catches Phil off guard and finally snaps a shot of him. "He would have broken my camera, except that I anticipated what he was up to," says Krupnick to the other reporters. Lee is referring to Phil moving closer and closer to Lee's camera sitting on the table. But Lee intuits what Phil wants to do and keeps moving the camera out of his reach.

Reporters ask Phil about the secret notes that he passed to Lee while he was in jail, the topics of which were reported in yesterday's *Tulsa World*. "Pres and I exchanged those notes to give Lee Krupnick a chance to develop into a mastermind detective like Mr. Maddux."

Pres Cochran refuses to comment, except to say, "I'll do my talking on the witness stand, not in the newspapers."

Once the paperwork is complete, Burkdoll, Ferguson, and Wilkerson quickly escort Phil across the street. Phil, with his blue coat over his left arm, smokes a cigarette, while reporters and photographers surround him. They walk the two hundred feet from the courthouse to the sandstone jail building and up the four granite steps.

They promptly place Phil in a musty cell in the forty-six-year-old jail. The small cell is cold and bare, compared to the warm and comfortable private room he had in Tulsa. He is given five blankets and two bed sheets for his steel bunk, and the officers go through Phil's change of clothes and the magazines he brought with him from Tulsa.

The Pawnee County Jail
(courtesy of the Pawnee Historical Society)

The Pawnee County Jail.
(courtesy of The Gateway to Oklahoma History)

A mystery witness for the state, Mrs. Edna Harman, of 1312 South Quaker Avenue, approaches Dr. and Mrs. Gorrell about giving testimony, and they escort her downtown to the private office of County Attorney Holly Anderson. She says she has vital information for the prosecution that will aid in their case. After she tells her story, Anderson issues a subpoena for Mrs. Harman to testify in the case and tells reporters "she has information of importance to the state" but declines to disclose the nature of her statements.

"Only four people know what she will tell—she, Doctor Gorrell, Tom Wallace, assistant attorney, and myself," says Anderson. "If anything about her testimony gets out, I'll know where it came from. The state is entitled to one secret, and she's my secret."

Pawnee County courtroom where the trial will be held

Monday, February 11

- Day 1 of the Trial — Jury Selection -

Phil is up before 7 AM and has a hot breakfast of oatmeal, toast, and coffee in his cell. At 8:50 AM, Sheriff Burkdoll and jailor Marion Hamby escort Phil from the jail to the courthouse across the street. There are about a hundred people, mostly men and boys, in the plaza watching the trek, while the swarm of reporters and photographers gathers around Phil to ask him questions.

"Have a good night?" shouts a reporter. Phil doesn't answer. He looks tense but stays composed, while keeping his eyes in front of him during the two-hundred-foot walk to the courthouse.

Phil is taken to the third floor of the Pawnee County Courthouse, where jury selection will begin for the twelve men who will take part in the trial. In a last-minute ruling, Judge Hurst bars the photographers from the floor. He doesn't need a media circus while a jury is chosen. He also bans smoking in the courtroom during sessions. Prentiss Rowe for the state insists on seeking the death penalty, and James A. McCollum for the defense makes the case for a self-defense or an insanity plea. A few of the potential jurors voice their opinion against the death penalty and are dismissed from the courtroom. "Is the state ready?" asks Judge Hurst.

State attorney Holly Anderson stands and addresses the court. "Last Saturday we obtained evidence of an important witness. Unless council for the defense is willing to waive the notice on Mrs. O. L. Harman, I want to ask a continuance until tomorrow morning."

"Does that mean you want to postpone the case?" asks Stuart of the defense. He's wearing a dark gray suit, a light-colored shirt, and a striped tie, as he stands to face Anderson.

"I only want to protect the state by proper notice unless the defense stipulates that the state may use Mrs. Harman and Preston Cochrane as witnesses without the customary two days' notice to the other side."

"We'll waive it," says Moss, as he takes his seat.

It's 9:15, and Judge Hurst orders the "venire men" (the panel of prospective jurors) to be sworn in. (Note: During this time in Oklahoma, only men were allowed to serve on juries. Women were not eligible to serve as jurors until 1952. The last state to allow women to be jurors was Mississippi in 1968. *The U.S. Women's Jury Movements and Strategic Adaptation: A More Just Verdict*, by Holly J. McCammon, pg. 38.)

The potential jurors rise, and Mrs. Nora Harshbarger, the district court clerk, administers the oath.

The first peremptory challenge begins with Rowe for the state. He wants to ensure that everyone on the jury will decide the case fairly and disregard the fact that the defendant is the son of a federal judge. He also wants to know if they have any fixed opinions of the case or whether their familiarity with the case, such as what has been printed in the newspapers, will affect their judgment. He asks if any prospective jurors have a problem with the death penalty. Some men are dismissed, based on their answers, and others are let go due to health reasons.

The defense begins its first peremptory challenge, then dismisses another venire man and replaces him. The state begins its second peremptory challenge, subsequently dismissing another venire man. Someone else takes his place, with further questioning by the state attorney. The defense begins its second challenge.

Just after a short recess, taken at 10:30, Rowe begins the sixth peremptory challenge and asks the prospective jury panel whether "hosiery salesmen" have visited their homes, but no one speaks up. He then asks whether anyone knows Frank Kendall, a former street department worker for the city of Tulsa and a part-time private investigator, or a man named W. N. Maben, a Tulsa attorney. Again, no one speaks from the panel. Yet one venire man says that a "salesman" called on him four days earlier and wanted his opinion about the trial. He gives a description of the man to the court.

The state attorneys have heard from reliable sources in the previous two weeks that someone is tampering with the prospective jury panel. Rowe is looking to discover whether Kendall or Maben are spreading propaganda that Phil is "crazy as hell" to aid the defense team.

From across the courtroom, Floyd Moss jumps out of his seat and shouts his objection to Prentiss Rowe's question to the prospective jurors. "I resent that! The state is just bringing this in because Mr. Maben is a friend of mine. This is just a nasty, dirty, unwarranted insinuation. Mr. Maben is right here in this courtroom and is a member of the Tulsa bar and in as good standing as Mr. Rowe of Pawnee County." Then he adds, "If they want to get rough, let's put the sawdust on the floor and go to it."

Judge Hurst suddenly stops the proceedings and orders the prospective jury panel to recess. He calls the attorneys from both sides to his chambers and closes the door to launch his own investigation into the state's tampering allegations. The prosecution suspects that William N. Maben, a close friend of Judge Kennamer, has been attempting to contact the fifty-one venire men. Maben's checkered past has raised some questions about his involvement in the Kennamer trial.

William N. Maben was a former Pottawatomie County district judge and a powerful political figure in the city of Pawnee and in Pottawatomie County. He was the first judge elected to the 10th Judicial District in Pottawatomie and Lincoln counties just after Oklahoma gained statehood. Later, he was indicted for misconduct in office by a grand jury in a special investigation made by the city of Shawnee and Pottawatomie County officials. Judge Maben was later indicted for accepting bribes from bootleggers and gamblers. He was suspended from office in April 1909 and later resigned as district judge.

Maben was also accused of releasing a convict by obtaining a forged appeal bond. He contends that he didn't know the bond was a forgery, and there was no evidence ever connecting the judge to the crime. Yet Justice Monroe Osborn issued an opinion that Maben lacked care and discretion in keeping the high office of attorney and recommended to the State Bar Board of Governors that Maben be disbarred. The Supreme Court overruled it on December 5, 1933.

William N. Maben
He may have been tampering with the witnesses and the jury

Judge Hurst and the attorneys remain behind closed doors for thirty minutes until Judge Hurst calls for Bailiff Trees to escort Mr. Maben to his chambers. Ten minutes later, Maben leaves the building and is not seen again. Reporters pounce on the attorneys, asking them what happened in the judge's chambers, but they, like the judge, refuse to divulge what was said in that private conference. Was Maben the attorney whom Anderson referred to on January 13 when he said that witnesses . . . and now the jury . . . were being tampered with by a Tulsa attorney? If so, what did Maben have to gain? We will never know.

At 11:40, Rowe turns the questioning over to the defense and James A. McCollum. McCollum questions the venire men about whether they have any prejudices against entering a plea of insanity and giving the benefit of the doubt if someone has a mental condition that prevents him from knowing right from wrong. McCollum also asks the men whether they have any prejudices toward a self-defense plea. After a lunch recess, McCollum continues his questioning. A few of the men are dismissed and replaced with new venire men.

At 2:37 PM and after eight peremptory challenges, the final juror is chosen from fifty-one venire men for the Kennamer trial. The jury panel consists of:

Ray Davidson, fifty, a married Pawnee farmer;

Noah Miller, forty-five, a filling station operator living near Pawnee, with four children;

Burnell F. Cave, forty-two, a wholesale gasoline dealer;

Every M. Easley, forty-five, a married farmer with two children;

Raymond Allen, thirty-four, a filling station operator, married with two children;

Richard E. Klutsenbeker, fifty, a married Pawnee lumber dealer with three children;

Jacob Clark, a married farmer with one child;

Leonard C. Mueller, thirty-seven, a bank clerk;

Ralph Dollarhyde, fifty-five, a married Pawnee farmer with three children;

Samuel B. Cameron, fifty-one, a filling station operator;

W. O. Cox, forty-seven, married with one child; and

Walter E. Kelley, a married stockman with five children.

The twelve men who will decide the fate of Phil Kennamer

Top row: (l to r) Ralph Dollarhyde, Ray Davidson, Richard Klutsenbeker,
Noah Miller, Burnell Cave, and Every Easley.
Bottom row: (l to r) Jacob Clark, Leonard Mueller, Raymond Allen,
Samuel Cameron, W. O. Cox, and Walter Kelley

Tuesday, February 12

- Day 2 of the Trial — Opening Remarks -

Tom Wallace, a veteran attorney for the state and a member of Holly Anderson's team, begins his opening remarks at 3:10 PM.

"Your Honor and gentlemen of the jury, I will read to you this information and make a statement as to what the evidence will be on behalf of the state." Wallace goes on for an hour describing Phil's childhood and the sequence of events that begin in 1934 and lead up to the night of the murder, including the two fatal wounds in Gorrell's head. He describes how Phil turned himself in to the authorities and admitted to the murder of John Gorrell.

Wallace intends to prove that Phil killed John Gorrell in the Forest Hills subdivision in Tulsa on Thanksgiving night with two gunshots to the head; that Phil was the one who proposed to kidnap Virginia Wilcox and extort $20,000 ransom; that the murder may have been left unsolved if Huff had not reported Kennamer's threat to kill Gorrell to the Kansas City police; that Phil threatened John on Thanksgiving Day and was disarmed by Beebe Morton; that Phil asked Sidney Born to take him to St. John's Hospital for the meeting with John; and that there was no struggle between Phil and John in the car on the night of the murder.

In closing, Wallace says, "When we have shown this, gentlemen, if the facts and evidence turn out as we have told you, then we shall expect a verdict of guilty at your hands with the extreme penalty. If the facts are shown as we have outlined them to you, we shall expect it."

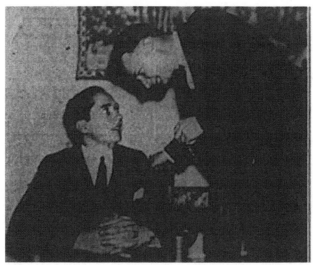

Richard Oliver (l) is talking with prosecution attorney Holly Anderson (r)
(Courtesy of the *Tulsa World*)

Wednesday, February 13

- Day 3 of the Trial — Testimony Begins -

On the first day of testimony, county attorney Holly Anderson calls **Dr. Gorrell** to the stand. The fifty-three-year-old doctor briefly describes John's life in a slow, clear voice when asked by Anderson.

"When did you last see your son alive?" asks Anderson.

"At 7:30 o'clock Thanksgiving night last year."

"Is your son now living or dead?"

"He's dead," replies the doctor dejectedly.

The defense team chooses not to cross-examine Doctor Gorrell, and he is dismissed.

The prosecution calls **Richard "Dick" Oliver** to the stand. He is a native of Tulsa and the roommate of John Gorrell.

"What was the occasion of your meeting Kennamer?" asks Anderson.

"John introduced him to me. He called him 'Bob Wilson.' That was in Kansas City. I think about November 20th. I later learned Wilson's true name was Kennamer."

Anderson then asks Dick, "Is the man who was introduced to you as Bob Wilson in the courtroom?"

Richard replies, "Yes," and points a steady arm at Phil.

Oliver also testifies that the next time he saw Phil was on the train at the Chelsea train station on his way to Tulsa to aid the authorities in the case.

Attorney Flint Moss begins his cross-examination by attacking John's character: "Gorrell was supposed to work at a switchboard in your hotel at Kansas City, wasn't he?"

"Yes," replies Dick.

Moss's attempts to show how John was intoxicated failed after many sustained objections by the state.

"Wasn't he so tight that you had to work there for him?"

The state's objection is sustained.

Moss begins another line of questioning by asking Dick what John had told him about Wilson.

"You say Gorrell introduced you to Kennamer [*sic—"Kennamer to you"] as 'Wilson' and told you he was the man he had told you about?"

"Yes," replies Oliver.

Moss: "What he told you was that the fellow was a Chicago gangster, wasn't it?"

"No."

"What had he told you?"

"John told me to notice him and remember him because if 'I ever get killed or murdered, that's the man who did it.'"

Surprised, Attorney Moss realizes that Oliver's answer does not help his case, and he quickly ends his cross-examination.

Oliver is dismissed from the stand.

Prosecuting Attorneys

Holly Anderson   **J. Berry King**

Floyd J. Huff, the aircraft mechanic from Kansas City, is called to the stand. Anderson asks whether he knew Gorrell and how he met Kennamer. Huff replies that he was already acquainted with Gorrell before his death. He met Kennamer at the Fairfax airport when Gorrell and Kennamer were trying to rent a plane. When they couldn't, due to the inclement weather, Huff gave them a ride back to Kansas City Municipal Airport.

He describes the drive to Tulsa with Phil, when Phil explained that he was renting the plane to kill Gorrell. Since that plan had been unsuccessful, Phil took out his knife and the extortion note and displayed them to Huff, detailing his new plan to kill Gorrell. Phil expressed his love for Virginia and said he was going to kill Gorrell to prevent the kidnapping. Floyd states that when he read of John's death, he immediately notified the authorities in Kansas City.

On cross-examination, Moss attempts to show that Floyd Huff is an unreliable witness, due to his criminal past; that both Floyd and Phil were drunk when Phil was describing his plots against John; and that Phil was insane at that time. Moss is unsuccessful.

Moss questions Huff about their drinking, the playing of craps, and the drive back to Tulsa. Moss goes back to an earlier statement Floyd made describing how Phil proposed to rent the plane and to parachute out of it after knocking John unconscious.

Aviator Floyd Huff
Gave Phil a ride back to Tulsa

"Have you ever heard of a man killing another man that way before?"

Dixie Gilmer, of the state, objects to the question, but Judge Hurst overrules the objection.

Moss asks Floyd if he believes that this form of homicide could be perpetrated. The state's objection is sustained.

Moss wants to show that Phil is no pilot and has had no experience in parachuting. As such, Phil could not execute such a plot to kill John Gorrell.

After the cross-examination, Moss turns the witness back to Anderson, who has no further questions, and the court dismisses Huff after his almost two-hour stint on the witness stand.

The next witness, **Ted Bath**, twenty-one, is called to the stand, and Anderson asks whether he was acquainted with John Gorrell.

"I was a good friend and a pallbearer at his funeral," says Ted, who lives at 1222 South Cheyenne Ave in Tulsa and is currently unemployed.

Ted Bath, a witness for the prosecution

Anderson asks, "Did you have a conversation with Gorrell and Kennamer?"

Moss objects and calls Anderson to the bench for a whispered conversation with the judge.

The court instructs Ted to answer the question.

"Yes," comes the response.

Ted tells of the conversation that he, John, and Phil had at the Brown Derby Café that September night, while he was on vacation from his work in Longview, Texas.

He describes Phil's idea to commit a robbery of a local beer parlor and how it was also Phil's idea to take compromising photos of Virginia Wilcox. Ted says that he wasn't interested in either of those ideas. Across the room, Phil becomes visually upset and clenches and releases his fists several times. He lowers his head, while his mouth is quivering.

Attorney Moss cross-examines Ted Bath: "Do you know Preston Cochrane, son of a Tulsa attorney and Phil's close friend?"

"Yes," replies Ted.

"Do you know Pat Burgess, a reporter from the *Tulsa World*?"

"I do not."

"Did John Gorrell introduce him to Cochrane and Burgess as 'my strong-arm man from Texas'?"

The state's objection is sustained.

Mr. Moss has no further questions. Ted is excused from the witness stand, and the court orders lunch recess.

After lunch, the courtroom fills to capacity, with the largest number of spectators yet, anticipating the mystery witness to be called next by the state. **Mrs. Edna Harman** is called to the stand, is sworn in, and states her name and address, 1312 Quaker Avenue, where she lives with her husband and three children. She is a leasing agent for the apartment house that she and her husband managed for the last fifteen years and where they now reside.

"Do you know Phil Kennamer?" asks Anderson.

Edna turns to the judge and says, "Honorable Judge, I'm afraid to testify because my life has been threatened, and my family has been threatened with death several times in the last twenty-four hours. I can't do it. My children mean more to me than anything else on earth. I'll take the penalty. I won't testify."

Attorney Moss quickly stands and encourages the witness to continue her testimony. "That's not the reason. She's not afraid. Let her tell all. I have no secrets. "

Anderson shouts at Mrs. Harman to be silent. The jurors are in shock, as are the courtroom spectators, who begin whispering. Judge Hurst raps his gavel for order.

"I didn't know this woman would talk like this. I never saw her till last Saturday," retorts Anderson, as he turns to the judge.

"The jury is admonished to disregard entirely the statement made by her and Mr. Moss," says Judge Hurst.

"I demand that a mistrial be declared immediately on the grounds of prejudice! Will you on pass my motion to declare a mistrial?" declares Moss, addressing the judge.

"It's the truth, Mr. Moss. It's the truth!" shouts Harman.

Judge Hurst raps his gavel again and sends the jury out of the courtroom and says, "I want the reporter to read to me, in private, what has been said."

Anderson angrily walks over to Moss. "What the hell! Is this planned?" Then, addressing the judge, he requests a ten-minute recess.

Defense attorney A. Flint Moss

The excited spectators begin talking loudly and fail to heed the rap of the gavel for order. Phil appears unaffected by the disruption. The judge makes another attempt to control the courtroom, which slowly begins to quiet down, and order resumes.

The reporter reads to the court what happened.

"You're nuts!" Moss shouts back at Anderson in a loud whisper heard ten feet away.

"Mr. Moss, the court stopped her and then you asked that it go on the record," says the annoyed judge, interrupting Moss.

"Please, Your Honor. Don't take advantage of my excitement," says Moss in consternation.

Attorney Dixie Gilmer stands and says, "Your Honor, he never was excited in his life!"

Prosecuting attorney W. F. "Dixie" Gilmer

"She endeavored to sell her testimony to the defendant," responds Moss.

"Mr. Moss, you're a liar!" shouts Mrs. Harman.

Moss tells the court he can prove it by contacting attorneys Maurice A. Breckinridge and Samuel A. Boorstin, both of Tulsa, who will confirm that Edna Harman attempted to sell her testimony in a case several years earlier for $2,500.

". . . and then $1,200 to sell her testimony to Judge Kennamer in this case. We can show some letters written to Judge Kennamer written by her. I can prove she called [attorney] Wash Hudson and told his [sic—"him"] she was a witness in a manslaughter case and asked how much she could charge."

"You're lying," says Harman, directing her statement at Moss and slowly shaking her head.

"The state told the jury what she will testify. That is false. I want to tell you what we know and then ask the county attorney to withdraw from the opening statement that part about her," continues Moss.

"It would be necessary if she doesn't testify," says Judge Hurst in agreement.

"Your Honor, she told me two minutes before the session opened that she would testify," states Attorney Dixie Gilmer.

"She told me she was threatened," says attorney Tom Wallace. "At noon, she got a phone call, and when she came back she was nervous. Two men told her to get out of town."

Anderson chimes in with "I got in touch with her Saturday. She told me a story that sounded plausible. I had every reason to believe she was telling a straightforward story. I vouch for her as I would for any other witness. If she's not telling the truth, I don't want her to testify."

"Let me help you," says Moss. "Call Boorstin, M. A. Breckinridge, Wash Hudson. They'll tell you."

"Mr. Wallace made a statement we want to challenge. He said this woman was approached by a lawyer she believed represented the defendant," says Stuart, of the defense team.

"I'll let her tell who he was," responds Wallace.

Mr. Coakley tells the court that once their team learned of the new witness, Edna Harman, he sent two representatives to talk with her, which "we were entirely proper in doing," once they were served with notice that the state was going to have her testify.

"This is not a police court. It is a court of justice, and I want my rights!" demanded Mr. Stuart.

"Mr. Moss, if the court will admonish the jury to disregard her statement here and the state takes her out of the opening statement, will you waive your motion?" asks the judge.

"I'm not certain the case isn't prejudiced by what has happened," came the reply.

"We'll recess twenty minutes, and Anderson can make an investigation."

Earlier in the day, while talking with a reporter, Edna Harman said that at first the threats were directed at her not to testify. Then the threats turned to harming her children. "They've told me that it would happen within thirty days after the trial. I know the men who came to see me. And if I am asked, I shall tell their names from the witness stand," said a defiant Harman.

"I'm not afraid for myself, but I am afraid for my children. The threats have mostly been toward my son, who carries the mail. It would be awfully easy some dark night for there to be an accident on the road from Tulsa to Ponca City," she continued.

In the lobby of the Pawnee Hotel, a reporter asked if she was the same Edna Harman who appeared as a witness in the B. O. Shepherd trial.

She simply smiled and said, "What's your next question?"

(The murder trial took place in 1930, and Wash Hudson was Shepherd's attorney. Hudson confirms during the short recess that Mrs. Harman was a witness in that trial.)

"Are you not the same Mrs. Harman who offered evidence in another trial in Tulsa some years before that?" asked the reporter.

She smiled again and said, "What are your next questions?"

"What other trials have you appeared in?"

"I would rather not answer those questions until I reach the witness stand."

"The defense attorneys will ask you then."

"I'm not sure that I shall take the stand. To tell the truth, I'm afraid. I've had all kinds of threats to keep me from the stand. Saturday, two men came to my house and suggested that I leave town before the subpoena reached me."

After further investigation, it is learned that Edna Harman contacted the Kennamer home and talked to Phil's sisters, Opal and Juanita, and told them that a young man rented an apartment from her, but it was not Phil. Was she willing to say that John Gorrell rented a room from her and she overheard him threatening to kill Phil, strengthening the case of self-defense? We will never know what testimony she was offering. But her intent was to help Phil's case and be remunerated for it.

Mr. Moss is fully aware of her history of selling testimony and refuses to use Mrs. Harman as a witness. But if Edna were to testify for the state, Moss would have the sisters be ready to take the stand to discredit any of her testimony, because they had been approached to buy her testimony. This could potentially devastate the credibility of the state's case.

Court reconvenes at 2:35 p.m. Lee Johnson, representing the state's staff of lawyers, stands to deliver a statement:

"As a citizen of Pawnee County, as members of the bar and prosecutors, I and my associates make the following statement with reference to the appearance of Mrs. Harman:

We regret what you heard and saw, and we want you to know we acted in good faith. It was not till Saturday that we learned she was willing to testify as we outlined." [Johnson then reads the opening statement that Edna Harman was going to testify that Phil rented a room from her and overheard Phil say, "That fellow's gotten yellow, he's backed out, and I'll go to Kansas City and put the skids under him," referring to Gorrell.]

"She related her story to the county attorney and he accepted it. No one knew she would make the scene. We now repudiate her and her testimony in the case. What her motives are, we cannot say. We desire to be fair and honorable. We now say the facts we expected to prove are untrue. I request on behalf of Anderson and Carl McGee, county attorney of Pawnee, that she be held for investigation by those two prosecutors.

Anderson stands and says, "Your Honor, we've been misled. We're acting in good faith. I don't feel we should go to trial now. I think we're entitled to a mistrial ourselves."

There is contentious discussion between the two sides for several minutes about calling a mistrial. Judge Hurst turns and asks, "Gentleman of the jury, is there a man on the jury who would be influenced by all this? If so, hold up your hand."

No hands go up.

"You tell me you will not be influenced, then. Are any of you now prejudiced to either side as a result of this?"

All the men respond with a resounding "No."

"In view of that, I'm going to order the trial to proceed. Mrs. Harman is to be held for investigation into direct contempt."

And with that, Mrs. Edna Harman is escorted to the Pawnee jail by Deputy Sheriff Jim Wilkerson. Her bail is set at $1,000.

Judge Hurst asks Anderson to call his next witness.

Edna Harman
She refuses to testify

Mrs. Gorrell is called to the stand by the state and testifies for ten minutes. Mr. Anderson gently asks many types of questions about the phone calls to the Gorrell home, in which the caller requested to speak to her son, John. The state claims that Phil made the numerous calls to the Gorrell residence. Mrs. Gorrell wipes her nose as she answers and is then dismissed from the stand without cross-examination by Mr. Moss. He knows it's not necessary to upset Mrs. Gorrell any more than she already is.

Eunice Word, the student nurse at St. Johns Hospital, is called to the stand and testifies about her activities on the night of the murder. She says that John Gorrell brought her to the hospital at 10:50 PM, ten minutes before her curfew. Moss briefly cross-examines her, and the Huntsville, Alabama, native is excused from future appearances.

Jack Snedden is called to the stand. Holly Anderson confirms that Jack knows Phil and Virginia and that Jack drove Phil to the Municipal Airport for Phil's flight to Kansas City.

Anderson asks Jack to speak about the night of the murder: how Phil had Jack read the extortion note and talked of killing John Gorrell with the knife he had in his coat pocket.

Jack says that he tried talking Phil out of going to his 11 PM meeting with John. Jack told Phil to think about his parents and the trouble he would cause. But Phil wouldn't listen, and a frustrated Jack walked away. It was 10:30 to 10:45 when Phil left the tavern.

Flint Moss cross-examines Jack. He establishes that Jack knew Phil for six or seven years and that Phil had threatened Jack with harm if he ever spoke ill of Virginia Wilcox. Even though Jack was currently dating Virginia, Phil expressed his continued love for her.

Moss asks, "How many times did he tell you he was in love with Virginia?"

"I did not count them," replies Jack.

"I know you didn't, Jack. But please be kind enough to us and the court and the jury and tell us."

"Well, an awful lot of times."

"Now, then, Jack, did he ever tell you a thing like this: that there was no use of him living? Virginia did not care about him and that that was all in living for him, that that was all worth an effort or thought?"

The state's objection is overruled.

"Yes, he did."

Moss asks Jack about the 1933 Christmas Dance on the 16th floor of the Mayo Hotel, where Phil, apparently drunk, walked on the ledge partway around the building before coming back into the room.

The High Hat Club, of which Jack is a member, is also a topic and how Phil tried to influence whomever he could to go to a dance with Virginia.

Moss finishes his cross-examination questions for the day, and Judge Hurst adjourns the court.

The state concludes its case without proving Phil's motive for the murder of John Gorrell but did show that Phil threatened to kill John, committed the crime, and then confessed to the murder. Now he must be punished.

Thursday, February 14

- Day 4 of the Trial — More Testimony -

The courthouse opens at 8 AM. The courtroom fills rapidly, just before **Jack Snedden** resumes his testimony at 9 AM. Flint Moss calls Jack to the stand to finish his cross-examination and asks Jack whether he knows John Gorrell. Jack tells the court that he does not.

Jack testifies that he is a frequent visitor at the Kennamer home and that Phil is a frequent visitor to the Snedden home. He recalls the night Phil came to the Owl Tavern and showed him the extortion note.

Dixie Gilmer wishes to ask some questions and holds the extortion note, Exhibit 2, in front of Jack, asking him whether the letter is in the handwriting of Phil Kennamer.

"This is not Phil's writing," Jack replies.

"I misunderstood you, then. It positively is not Phil Kennamer's handwriting and the note is not his handwriting?"

"Yes, sir."

"Of course, you don't know whose handwriting it is?"

"No."

Jack recalls how Phil told him a few times a week how much he loved Virginia.

"The drunker he was, the more he would say that he loved her," says Jack.

Gilmer reads the jury the letter that Phil had written to Virginia. Phil becomes embarrassed, lowers his head, and covers his eyes with his right hand. Phil had given that letter to Jack to mail but now knows Jack never mailed it.

Randall "Beebe" Morton, a young heavy-set Osage Indian, now a student at Kansas University, is called to the stand at 10 AM. Beebe lives at 1344 South Peoria. Tragically, both of his parents, Charles and Mary Morton, were shot and killed by a neighbor at their home just a few years earlier. He testifies about his meeting with Phil Kennamer on Thanksgiving night. Phil showed him the knife and the extortion note he'd never mailed. Phil professed his love for Virginia and said that he was going to kill John Gorrell to protect her from the extortion plot. Beebe tells of how he took the knife from Phil, gave it back, and then took it from him again after having second thoughts.

Jake Easton, a red-haired student at Oklahoma University, is called to the stand at 10:15 AM and testifies how he overheard Phil ask Sidney Born for a ride at the Quaker Drug Store the night of the murder.

Mary Jo Hafford, the waitress at the Quaker, is called to the stand at 10:30 AM and confirms Jake's testimony. She also says that she later saw Sidney outside the drugstore on Thanksgiving evening at 11:15 PM.

Mary Jo Hafford, waitress at the Quaker

Wesley Cunningham takes the stand 11:10 AM and explains how he found John's body at Victor and Forrest, told his stepfather, and called the police. He describes that area of the neighborhood where John's car was parked, facing northwest, with the left front tire over the curb.

John G. Tucker, a Tulsa detective, who was first on the murder scene, testifies at 11:30 AM that no one touched the body, and he stayed at the scene until Sergeant Maddux arrived thirty minutes later.

Sergeant Henry Maddux is called next to take the stand at 11:35 AM. Mr. Gilmer shows two photos that Maddux took of Gorrell's body: one from the passenger side of the car and a close-up of the two bullet holes in Gorrell's head. Both Dr. and Mrs. Gorrell begin to cry. A friend escorts Mrs. Gorrell, weeping, out of the courtroom. The photos continue to make their way to the jurors, who study them carefully. Detective Maddux says that he took the picture of Gorrell's body "to the right of the front door" at the crime scene. The photo of the head wounds was taken at the morgue.

Maddux is questioned extensively on his treatment of the evidence, including whether he found any fingerprints on the gun. He testifies that none were found, that someone had successfully removed the prints.

The defense contends that there was a violent struggle between Phil and John just before the gun was fired. The picture that Maddux took at the scene shows that neither John's clothing nor his hair was in disarray, which would indicate evidence of a struggle. John's body did not have any contusions or abrasions either, which would point to a struggle, thus landing a blow to the defense's theory of self-defense.

Dr. Carl Simpson of Tulsa is called to the stand to establish the state's "corpus delecti." The purpose of his testimony is to prove that a crime has occurred beyond a reasonable doubt before a person can be convicted of that crime. In this case, Dr. Simpson testifies that John Gorrell was killed by two bullets to the head. Even though Phil Kennamer confessed out of court to the murder and turned himself in to the authorities, he cannot be convicted solely on his own confession.

The defense does not cross-examine Dr. Simpson.

The court calls for a lunch recess at 11:45.

Court reconvenes at 1:30 PM, and Henry Maddux is recalled to the stand for cross-examination by defense attorney Flint Moss. Detective Maddux was asked by one of Phil's defense attorneys, C. A. Coakley, about some aspects of the case during the lunch recess. Maddux refuses to discuss them, saying, "I told Mr. Coakley the state would bring out all the facts in the case, and the witness stand was the proper place for me to talk."

The state introduces the pistol and the fatal bullets found at the scene as exhibits for both the state and the defense.

Deputy Sheriff Nate Martin is called to the witness stand at 2:20 PM and testifies that he first met Phil on December 1, when Phil turned himself in and admitted that he killed John Gorrell.

The state rests its case at 2:44 PM.

Defense attorney A. Flint Moss begins his opening statement at 3:05 PM. He spends the next fifty-five minutes describing Phil as "erratic, eccentric, peculiar, brilliant . . . a youth with no mental stability or equilibrium."

"In the language of the street, Phil couldn't take it. He killed Gorrell because he was goaded to save the girl of his dreams from harm. He exposed the extortion plot of John Gorrell. It was Gorrell's plot, and we shall prove it."

Moss's strategy for his line of defense is to spend about 75 percent of his time showing the court that Phil is insane and the rest of the time that the murder was in self-defense. His witness list consists of those who have known Phil over the past years and will testify to Phil's odd behavior to build the case for Phil's insanity. This task should be easier than proving the self-defense plea. Even with Phil's admission to the murder, it is Moss's hope that either one or both of his defense strategies will get Phil off with a lighter sentence.

At 4 PM, court is recessed for the day.

Friday, February 15

- Day 5 of the Trial — Defense Witnesses -

Before court resumes this morning, Phil is across the street from the courthouse, getting a shave in the Midway Barbershop, while his friends Robert Thomas, Allen Mayo, and Claude Wright joke and laugh with him. It's the first time he's been able to see or talk to them since he has been in jail.

"Just wait until I get on the stand," says Phil. "I'll tell the world something they never heard about you guys before, and believe me, I know a lot about each of you. But don't worry. Never mind. Everyone says I'm crazy. Say, this guy Jack Snedden is sure my pal. First, he steals my girl. And I wrote Virginia a letter last August and gave it to Jack to mail, and he just keeps it until now and then turns it over to the prosecution."

"Are you sore at Jack, Phil?" asks Claude.

"No, not sore. He is just a nut, like me. But can he go around and make trouble. My pal, Jack."

Phil is talking and laughing so much that the barber has trouble shaving him and keeping the lather out of Phil's mouth.

"I wish I had my school books with me, and you could help me with my studies," says Claude.

"No, no. I'm crazy now and couldn't help you a bit," Phil replies sarcastically, referring to his attorney's line of defense.

And with that, the crowded barbershop roars with laughter.

Then Phil gets serious. He pulls himself up in the barber's chair and addresses Thomas. "You had the nerve saying I told you to come along and I would show you Gorrell's body. You know I didn't say that. Anyway, you were so drunk, you didn't know anything about what I said or did."

Thomas just smiles and shakes his head.

The barber finishes Phil's shave, then the sheriff grabs Phil by the arm and whisks him out of the barbershop and across the street to the courthouse.

At 9 AM, the flying instructor at the Spartan School of Aeronautics, **Jess Green**, is called to the stand. He tells the court that John Gorrell took flying lessons from February to August of 1933. Flint Moss introduces the twelve flying reports that John filled out, then hands them to Jess. Moss asks Jess if the handwriting on the slips is John's.

"I couldn't say. To be absolutely correct, there might be some changes."

Judge Kennamer takes the stand at 9:20 AM, and Moss offers into evidence a letter written by Phil, with a comment that he has never read it, and asks the witness, "Is this your son's handwriting?"

On hearing that remark, King jumps to his feet and shouts, "Do you mean you are offering evidence you haven't even read?"

"Don't be surprised at anything I do," Moss says quietly.

"It is," says Judge Kennamer, confirming to Moss that it was his son's writing.

Moss then hands the judge the extortion note and envelope. "Is that in your son's handwriting?"

Judge Kennamer looks at the note, then puts his glasses to see it more closely. "My judgment is it's not his handwriting."

"That's all. You may cross-examine."

"No examination," replies Dixie Gilmer.

At 9:25 AM, **J. Curtis Shearman,** a handwriting expert from Wichita, Kansas, is called to the stand. Moss asks many questions to successfully qualify Shearman as an expert in handwriting analysis. Then he hands the witness some slips signed by Gorrell from flying lessons and the extortion note and asks, "When was it that these were submitted to you for examination?" He leans, relaxed, against the jury box.

Shearman answers that he saw them in December after he was called by Moss.

Gilmer suddenly rises. "If the defendant is seeking to prove Gorrell wrote the extortion note, we will admit it."

"You say you admit that the handwriting on the envelope and the two pages of the letter is that of Gorrell's?"

"Yes," replies Gilmer.

Moss hands the note to the jurors to pass around and tells them to observe the fact that the word *death* is emphasized and written differently, while the rest of the note is handwritten.

Claude Wright
(courtesy of The Gateway to Oklahoma History)

Claude Wright, nineteen, takes the stand at 9:30 AM. Claude is the son of the president of Sunray Oil Company of Tulsa and tells the court the strange things that Phil has done in the past. He describes how Phil constantly talked about his feelings toward Virginia Wilcox and about the few dates he had with her. Claude spoke of a letter that Phil received from Virginia and said Phil felt that he wasn't getting along very well with Virginia, because she didn't want to see him any more. Phil talked of having a final date with her, then committing suicide so that it would look like a hunting accident. Phil told Claude that he did not care to go on without Virginia's love.

Then Claude is asked about a time when Phil jumped from one moving car to another. He tells the court about an incident where Allen Mayo was driving back to Tulsa after midnight, and Phil was in the backseat.

"I was with Phil during one of our Christmas dances held at Oakhurst Country Club during the year 1930, I believe, coming back from the dance late at night. He had a date with a girl and Phil, as we drove up behind Jack Snedden, Phil said, 'I want to talk to Jack.' We drove up behind him, and Phil opened the door. I grabbed for him, but he was already through the door. Phil swung over onto that other car. We were driving about fifty-five or sixty miles per hour."

(Originally called the Golfer's Club Association when it was established in 1921, the 312-acre property was renamed Oakhurst Country Club after it was cleared of more than two thousand oak trees. The club was renamed Oaks Country Club in 1947, when its members purchased it from the association.)

In another incident in the fall of 1930, Claude tells of how he, Jack Snedden, and Phil were out at the Snedden farm. As Phil drove his Dodge sedan across a field, Claude and Phil were "fighting a little," and Claude was in the backseat.

"Phil was driving across this plowed field, which he had no business doing. I told him he was going too fast and told him to slow down. He told me it was none of my business how he drove his own car. I told him I did not have to keep quiet. He said he could stop me from talking. We got out of the car and had a fight."

When Claude is asked who won the fight, he says modestly, "I was on top of him," to which the courtroom responds with laughter.

After the fight, they got back into the car, and Phil began to drive fast again. He hit a ditch, and Claude bounced up, hitting the ceiling of the sedan. After a few days, Phil told Claude he was so angry that he'd thought of killing him. But Claude knew he didn't mean it.

Claude also testifies that in social gatherings, Phil would behave himself when he wasn't drunk. When he was drunk, he was usually asked to leave. According to Claude, Phil seemed to think he was smarter than everyone else. He used words that no one understood when he talked of politics, religion, or any subject.

Dixie Gilmer cross-examines Claude about the things Phil has done in the past. Gilmer seems to be successful in debunking the defense's argument that many of the crazy things Phil did are typical of a lot of boys his age.

"Do you think Phil is sane or insane right now?"

"I don't know just how to answer that. I can't make it any clearer."

J. Berry King leans over to Gilmer and asks in an undertone, "Has he been told what to say?"

Moss hears the question and objects.

"Did any juryman hear what I said? If so, I apologize," says King in sincerity.

One juror comments that he thought he did hear King's remark.

"I apologize," says King again.

The court is recessed for a short break and reconvenes at 11:30. **Allen Mayo**, nineteen, is called to the stand. He has known Phil for eight years. Flint Moss asks Allen to describe an incident that occurred on the 16th floor of the Mayo Hotel. In the hotel's large ballroom, a Christmas dance was held by a girl's sorority in 1933, with a couple hundred boys and girls in attendance. Phil had been drinking and climbed out a window, then walked very rapidly along the edge, starting on the south side and continuing on the west side of the building. He passed fifteen windows that are four feet wide with a two-and-a-half-foot-wide stone ledge. Phil had to grab the bricks to keep from falling when he passed each window. Jack tried to pull him back into the ballroom by his coat. He pulled Phil about halfway into one window, but Phil refused to come back and remained out on the ledge. Jack finally persuaded Phil to climb back into the ballroom through the window.

Where Phil Dared Death

The arrow points to the ledge on the Mayo hotel building upon which Phil Kennamer walked one night during a dance, according to the testimony yesterday of his Tulsa friends. This ledge, indicated by the white dotted line, is on the west side of the building. The defense offered the testimony of the hotel incident as proof of Phil's mental instability—terming his actions that of an insane youth.

According to testimony offered Tuesday at Pawnee, Phil reached the ledge through a window (shown at extreme left) and then walked south along to the ledge and around the corner, entering the ballroom at a point where the dotted line terminates.

Here is a photographer's "view" of the narrow ledge on the west side of the Mayo hotel where witnesses said Phil Kennamer, federal judge's son, walked one night in a daredevil stunt during a dance at the hotel.

A view of the ledge from the 16th floor of the Mayo Hotel where Phil took a walk

The Mayo Hotel, 115 West 5th Street
Downtown Tulsa, Oklahoma

During the time that Allen was dating Virginia, Phil told him just how to act when he went out with her. If Allen didn't do what he was told, he said Phil would "bump me off."

"Did Phil ever tell you of his intention to commit suicide?" asks Moss

"Yes."

"When?"

"About three years ago."

"Where?"

"At my home."

"Was anyone else there?"

"No."

"Tell the jury about it."

Allen tells the court that during the time he was dating Virginia, Phil had driven to Allen's home one evening, honked the horn, and asked him to come outside. After a short conversation, Phil told Allen that he was tired of living, he didn't have any friends, and his girl (Virginia Wilcox) didn't care for him. Phil said he was going to end it all by driving his car off a bridge.

Moss questions Mayo about Phil's state of mind. "Keeping in mind the things he said and done, is he a normal boy?"

"I don't think he is."

"So you think he's crazy?"

"I believe I'd say he was."

Gilmer steps up to cross-examine and asks Mayo whether Phil was drinking when he walked on the ledge of the sixteenth floor of the Mayo Hotel.

"Yes. Some."

"Now when did you first decide Phil Kennamer was insane?"

"I think a couple of years ago."

"Why did you fail to tell any authority, your parents, or someone that you thought something ought to be done?"

"What do you mean? About telling my folks? I did tell my folks about it."

"Did you tell them he was insane?"

"I told them he was slightly off."

The boys are frequent visitors at each other's homes. Allen says his mother, who also knows Phil, agrees. This testimony helps solidify Moss's insanity defense.

Gilmer asks "You think Phil Kennamer knows it's wrong to take human life?"

"It just depends on what state of mind the fellow is in."

Court is recessed for lunch.

After the lunch recess at 1:30 PM, seventeen-year-old **Homer Wilcox Jr.** is summoned to the stand. He states that he has lived in Tulsa all of his life and knows Phil well and has seen him frequently in the last two years.

"Homer, last fall did Phil Kennamer tell you of a plan on the part of the deceased John Gorrell to kidnap your sister?"

"Yes," replies Homer, nervously biting his lips.

"Are you able, Homer, to fix the date with certainty when Phil told you?"

"Yes. Between the tenth and fifteenth of October,"

"Tell why you are certain."

"Because I had seen a show at the Ritz Theater, and I found out when the show was there."

"You remember then that you and Phil had attended a certain show and it was then?"

"Yes."

"And you and your father checked the date of the show?"

"Yes."

"Now tell the jury just what Phil told you about the plot to kidnap your sister on the part of Gorrell."

"He told me that Gorrell was in a gang in Kansas City and that he had told him last summer of the plan to kidnap my sister, and he would prevent it at any cost."

""Homer, did he tell you what he would do if necessary to prevent it?"

"He said if necessary he'd kill Gorrell."

Homer also says that he did not see the extortion letter, nor did he divulge the kidnapping plot to his parents because he didn't believe it. Phil repeated this plot to Homer four or five times before the date of the murder.

He admits he pled guilty to shooting out the streetlights near the spot where Gorrell's body was later found but denies that he had anything to do with Gorrell's death.

Homer knew that Phil had gone to Kansas City and saw him only once, just a few days after he returned from the trip. They spoke briefly at the Mayo Hotel about his trip and about his seeing Gorrell. It was brief, as Homer describes it, because "I was with a friend, and the friend left and then came back," and then the conversation stopped.

"Didn't you leave town when you heard of Gorrell's death?" asks prosecution attorney Gilmer.

Homer answers that he went to Toledo for a week the day after Phil surrendered. When asked why, Homer responds, "Because Mother wanted to get Virginia out of town to avoid publicity, and I just went along." They left Sunday morning after Thanksgiving by train and returned the following week by plane.

Virginia Wilcox

Homer Wilcox Jr. (l) and Virginia Wilcox (r)

Virginia Wilcox follows her brother at 1:50 PM to the witness stand. She is modishly attired in a dark-blue suit marked by a luxurious platinum fox collar with points extending to her elbow. She is wearing a small dark-blue felt hat tilted over her right ear, with her dark wavy hair exposed on the left side of her head. Virginia's oval face holds a slight tinge of color, while her lips are a bright red. Her black-gloved hands are folded in her lap. Suspended around her neck by a thin gold chain is a small gold cross, which is barely noticeable to the jurors. Her expression is very intense and her emotions subdued. She creates a buzz when she enters the courtroom and makes no eye contact with Phil. The courtroom is dramatically quiet while she speaks in a low, sweet voice while testifying, and a couple of the jurors lean forward to hear her. For twenty-two minutes, Virginia testifies that she had met Phil about four years earlier. She received many letters and telephone calls during the last four years from Phil. "One time he asked me for a date, I think, two years in advance. I told him he could not."

Virginia is questioned about a phone conversation she had with Jack Snedden last August while she was at the family's vacation home in Michigan. "Jack wanted me to write a letter to him [Phil]. Said Phil was drinking very much, and I might be able to stop him." When asked if she wrote that letter, she says, "No." Later, Virginia wrote Jack a letter and told him that she could not do that. "I just couldn't see myself writing to Phil."

Virginia also testifies that Jack had told her about the plot to kidnap her, and, like her brother, she didn't tell her parents about it because she didn't believe it and didn't want to worry them. She did not know John Gorrell.

While she testifies, Kennamer keeps his hands over his eyes and his head bowed. He never once looks up, and she never looks at Phil. She says that she repelled Phil's advances and believes that he still loves her.

At 2:15 PM, a friend and neighbor, twenty-five-year-old **Lawrence Stewart** of 2205 Terwilleger, tells how he first met Phil in Santa Fe, New Mexico, in July 1931. Then later, as neighbors in Tulsa, Phil tried to convince him to go to Mexico with him and start a revolution.

"I think he was irrational," says Lawrence.

When asked if he thought Phil was insane, Lawrence responds, "I'm not in a position to say. He's temperamental and impulsive."

At 2:25 PM, Phil's sister, **Juanita Hayes**, describes Phil's incidents of running away from home and wanting to join the French Foreign Legion. He told his big sister how he wanted to go to any part of the world where there was trouble, to participate in it. Those areas included Cuba, Europe, South America, and China.

Phil also told her of his adoration of Virginia Wilcox, and he wanted his sister to keep his discussions with her private and not to be spoken of with the rest of the family. In an effort to prove Phil's insanity, the defense attorney asks about Phil's mental state in October and November, prior to the murder.

"There were a good many occasions on which Phil was easily disturbed, highly nervous, and he was in and out of the house, and we didn't have much opportunity to talk," says Juanita.

At 2:45 PM, **Judge Franklin Kennamer** is called to the stand and testifies for one hour and fifty minutes. Phil listens as his father begins to testify, and his attitude becomes that of a small boy. In describing Phil, the judge says, "Phil was a perfectly born baby—that is, physically. I would say that temperamentally his disposition is headstrong, and I have tried from his earliest childhood to correct that headstrong disposition. In other words, strong emotion was manifest in him. You could notice that when he was fourteen or fifteen, he seemed to almost skip the youthful period; he read everything he could get a hold of. He seemed to manifest above the ordinary child and has always been nervously temperamental. . . . He had a very emotional disposition; he would be high or very low. . . . No medium ground at all."

He testifies that Phil "was a heavy reader and learned to read early in life. Between the age of five and six years of age and just didn't seem to be interested in school. It wasn't high enough for him, and he wasn't getting along fast enough."

He tells of the incidents when Phil would run away to Texas, Florida, and California and twice to New York, only to be found and be brought home again. The judge told the court of his numerous attempts to interest Phil in some sort of profession or business venture. Phil would try his hand at different occupations, but they were all short lived.

Phil's father, Judge Franklin Kennamer

Phil's father never knew about Phil's love for Virginia or of his heavy drinking. On a trip to Alabama, Judge Kennamer describes how Phil was "very moody on that trip, very blue . . . thought that there was nothing for him. He thought he might just as well get out of the country.

"I always talked to him about taking these trips, running around over the country. I talked to him lots about that. As I remember it, it was [the] early part of the summer, I might be in error as to the exact date, I was sitting in my front room reading. It was Sunday afternoon, I think. Phil came into the room. I was sitting there alone reading. He was crying." At this point, Judge Kennamer stops and fumbles for his handkerchief. "He said he knew he had given me and his mother a lot of trouble, and he was sorry about it. Said he was going to take a trip." Mr. Kennamer stops and fumbles again. "I told him that I objected to these trips, running around over the country without knowing where you are going and what you are going to do. I told him they wouldn't get him any place. It was hard on your mother and me. He said he knew it worried us a lot; he was a lot of bother to us. 'You don't understand what kind of trip I'm going to take,' he said. 'I am going on one from which you never return.'" The gray-haired judge is unable to continue and begins to cry, removing his gold-rimmed glasses and drying his eyes with his handkerchief.

The courtroom crowd exhibits extreme sympathy for the judge, and many are crying as well. Phil sits ashamed and broken.

Attorney Moss asks the judge about the night of the murder. Phil had come home after everyone had eaten dinner. The judge told Phil to have his dinner. A short time later, after he ate dinner, Phil returned to the front room. According to the judge, "We were sitting there, in the front room. The room is rather large. I assume twenty feet long, probably fifteen feet wide. He came and was pacing the room rapidly and very nervous. I said, 'Phil, sit down and compose yourself and visit with us a while.' He walked over to my older boy; he was lying down on the couch. He had driven in from Oklahoma City and had a cold. Phil walked over to him and asked him to take him up to the drug store up near St. John's hospital. He said he didn't want to get out. Franklin told him he didn't want to go out on account of the cold he had. I finally said I am going up there to get some cigars, Phil, and I will take you up."

Working his angle to prove his insanity plea, Attorney Moss asks, "Keeping in mind all of these things that you have known about Phil through the years, Judge, which you have heretofore detailed and his conduct and demeanor during the fall of 1934, and keeping in mind to his conduct on the night when this killing took place, and acting upon the assumption that it did occur some time between 11:30 and 12:15, tell the jury whether or not, in your judgment, as you know your son Phil, whether or not he was rational or irrational?"

The judge responds, "I have no doubt he was irrational and irresponsible."

At 5 PM, court is recessed for the day.

In other news, Dr. Born tells reporters that "a few days after Sidney died, I started an investigation . . . which has shown us many things, none of which I think can be revealed at this point." He points to a large stack of reports and says, "All the evidence indicates Sidney's death was a case of homicide." Dr. Born has stated in the past that he has never been convinced that his son's death was a suicide but that it was murder. The information provided by his investigators has strengthened that belief.

Sheriff Garland Marrs is convinced that young Sidney was murdered. "I have had two men working on the case for several weeks but so far have uncovered no information that would point to guilt on the part of anyone connected with the Kennamer case.

We are still working, and I think eventually the murder will be solved."

One of the strongest indications of murder is the fact that Sidney had a large swollen spot on his right cheek, which appeared to have been the result of a blow to the face.

Saturday, February 16

- Day 6 of the Trial — More Defense Witnesses -

At 9 AM, Dr. Karl Menninger, a psychiatrist of Topeka, Kansas, describes his observations of Phil Kennamer. He establishes to the court that he received his degree from Harvard and has been practicing medicine since 1917. He has done postgraduate work in New York, Chicago, Boston, and Europe. He has been in contact with several thousand people who have nervous and mental diseases and is currently treating about sixty patients.

Dr. Menninger spent three to four hours with Phil at the jail in January. Attorney Moss reiterates the highlights from the previous testimony about Phil Kennamer's life for forty minutes. When he finishes, he asks Dr. Menninger, "Would you say the defendant is rational or irrational?"

The prosecution attorney, Berry King, objects because there is much in the hypothetical question that should be stricken and the drinking of Kennamer should be included.

Dr. Menninger says he is taking into consideration Phil's behavior, attitude, and emotional reactions in conversation; Phil's interpretation of himself, his general attitude toward others, and his overall psychological reactions; and the history of Phil's previous behavior.

The state wants Moss's hypothetical question reduced to stipulate only the facts. Court is recessed at 10 AM, so that counsel can seek to agree on a stipulated hypothetical question of facts, on which both sides will predicate the testimony of Dr. Menninger. It takes nearly three hours for both sides to come to an agreement about which evidence should be included in the question for the doctor: a letter Phil wrote to Virginia saying that he would drink himself to death, the walk on the outside ledge of the sixteenth-floor ballroom of the Mayo Hotel, and Huff's testimony about Phil's intent to kill John.

Court resumes at 12:56 PM, but there is no mention of the testimony that was heard before the recess and of posing the hypothetical question. Instead, former Oklahoma chief justice **Charles W. Mason** takes the stand. He testifies that Judge Kennamer called him two years earlier and asked for a favor. Both Mason and Judge Kennamer served together on the state Supreme Court bench for eight years. Judge Kennamer wanted Mason to interview Phil for a job in the office. Mason said he would. Phil called Mason, and the two met.

"He came to my office, and I told him to sit down. He seemed very calm, cool, and deliberate. He sat down a few minutes, and we discussed this work that he wanted to obtain. He then became very nervous, stood first on one foot and then the other, paced back and forth, and worked his way around my flat-topped desk while we were discussing the newspaper business. I suggested that probably he would be interested in police court to start with. I understood that he had a very vivid imagination and would probably like that work. He drifted over to the window—my office is on the sixteenth floor of the Petroleum Building—and in the course of my statement he said, 'This would be a fine place to commit suicide, wouldn't it? Jump out of here headfirst.'" Mason says he thought nothing of the comment at the time.

Phil then told Mason that he wouldn't be interested in the police court end of the business. Yet he did say he was interested in a statewide beer distributorship or building a brewery. Phil had a plan to talk to people to put up some money and make a million dollars in the next five years. Phil didn't expound on the idea, and Mason says he didn't ask. Phil also talked of buying a newspaper. Eventually, Mason did help Phil get employment in the office of Walter Harrison of the *Oklahoman* and *Times* newspapers.

During his one-and-a-half-hour visit with Mason, Phil discussed becoming a pilot and going to Central or South America to join a revolution. Then he'd become a good ruler of that country after the revolution. When Moss asks whether Mason thought Phil was rational, Mason says, "Well, he was highly nervous, and from the conversation at the time, in my opinion, I didn't think so."

Dixie Gilmer of the state begins his cross-examination of Mason. Gilmer's approach is like a dagger to the defense, piercing and demolishing Attorney Moss's carefully constructed argument. With regard to Phil's pacing in the judge's office, Gilmer asks Mason if he has observed Mr. Moss characteristically pace back and forth in a courtroom. Mason says he has. Gilmer asks if he thought there was anything particular in Mr. Moss doing it.

"You don't think that Mr. Moss is a little off, do you, Judge, on that account?" giving Moss a verbal dig.

An objection comes from the defense table, and the judge sustains it.

"Would the fact that Phil Kennamer walked back and forth make you think he was insane?" asks Gilmer.

"Not that in itself," replies Mason.

Gilmer asks Mason about Phil talking about buying a newspaper. "We will say he was seventeen years of age. Isn't that the normal, proper, ordinary reaction of a normal boy starting in at the bottom of a business to hope someday be at the head of that concern, isn't that right?"

"Yes, sir."

"That is what the conversation was, he was ambitious?"

"He was ambitious. Yes."

Gilmer now asks about Phil mentioning going into the beer business. "Just study for a moment or two and tell me how many different people with whom you came in contact wanted to get in the beer business at that time. There have been a lot of them, haven't there?"

Mason replies, "Not a lot, but I know that a lot of people did get in that business."

"Would anything in the fact that he wanted to get into the beer business lead you to believe that he was insane?"

"Probably not, but the fact that he wanted to build a brewery, which would cost a large sum of money, I thought that was a little odd."

Next, Gilmer asks about Phil's desire to become an aviator and go to Central America. "At one time in your lifetime you had the same desire and put [it] into effect, didn't you, all but serving in the revolution?"

"Yes, sir. I was anxious to serve in the United States Army and still am in the reserves."

"That was a normal reaction on your part, wasn't it?"

"I thought so."

"Is there anything in the fact that Phil Kennamer expressed a desire to become a pilot and to go to South America which would make you think he was insane?"

At this question, Mason finally has an answer that is not simply falling into the trap laid by Gilmer. "I don't know as it is a worthy desire to go to a foreign country and overthrow the government and become the ruler of that country. I don't think that is a worthy desire."

And finally, Gilmer asks, "If he hadn't killed that boy, they couldn't possibly drag you up here to testify that he is insane?"

"Probably not."

"You would not have come had it not been for that?"

"I probably would not."

Gilmer scores a victory for the prosecution.

Court is recessed at 1:22 PM until 9 AM Monday morning.

Sunday, February 17

The jury does not go to church today, by order of Judge Hurst, who fears that any of them could have contact with someone involved with the case. Instead, the jury is taken to Pawnee Bill's Old Town for a few hours of fun and entertainment. The rest of the weekend the men would read literature, excluding information about the Kennamer case, or play cards. (Note: Pawnee Bill was born Gordon William Lillie and was given the nickname after working as an interpreter with the Pawnee Indians in Buffalo Bill's wild west show. In 1888, he began his own show called "Pawnee Bill's Historic Wild West," with his wife, May. In 1908, Pawnee Bill and Buffalo Bill combined their shows, calling it the "Two Bills' Show," which was later foreclosed. Pawnee Bill and May opened "Pawnee Bill's Old Town" in 1930 near their buffalo ranch west of Pawnee, Oklahoma, selling Indian and Mexican arts and crafts. The venue consisted of log cabins, tepees, saloons, gunfights, and entertainment of the Old West, including an annual rodeo. The business burned to the ground in the 1940s and was never rebuilt. The home still stands and is now a museum filled with the original furnishings, located just west of the town.

Pawnee Bill died in his sleep in his Pawnee home in 1942 at the age of eighty-one.)

Monday, February 18

- Day 7 of the Trial — Phil Testifies -

As soon as the courthouse opens at 8 AM, it is mobbed by a stampede of spectators. They rush up the stairs to the third floor, in anticipation of Phil Kennamer's testimony today. Men and women alike are pushing and shoving their way to the courtroom, which is filled within three minutes.

"Hats were knocked off, slippers were lost, dresses were torn and feet trampled upon . . ."

Cursing, squeals, laughter, and shouts fill the air. The crowd crashes the courtroom doors, and Sheriff C. M. Burkdoll and five other deputies run in to clear the room. More than a hundred spectators stand in the rear of the room and along the walls. Even the corridor behind Judge Hurst's bench is packed with people. Another hundred people who could not get into the courtroom are moved to the second floor, with a deputy standing guard at the landing.

Judge Hurst issues orders that this morning, no one under the age of eighteen, including school children, will be admitted. Spectators carry chairs from the pressroom to place along the railing and in the aisles, leaving many reporters with nothing to sit on to do their work. When a chair is found vacant, the court's administrative staff and reporters claim it and, to avoid losing their seats when they must leave the room, carry the chairs with them, in and out of the courtroom. Strange new faces of individuals pretending to be reporters with pencil and paper take their places at the press tables. Judge Hurst orders Bailiff Mike Trees to remove those who are not bona fide reporters.

The seating capacity of the courtroom is 400, but today it contains no less than 500 people. Many of the principals and reporters are forced to use a private stairway from the first floor of the courthouse to the third-floor district court clerk's office to get past the mob of spectators.

Waiting to Hear Kennamer Testify

—Photo by Lee Krupnick, World Staff

Hundreds of persons thronged the entrance to the Pawnee county courthouse yesterday morning before the doors were opened to make sure that they obtained seats in order that they might clearly hear the words of Phil Kennamer as he told his story of the slaying in Tulsa last Thanksgiving of John F. Gorrell, jr. The above picture shows part of the crowd.

Crowd outside the Pawnee county courthouse

The photograph shows a section of the downtown district in Pawnee, seat of the Kennamer murder trial which begins Monday. Pawnee county's new $150,000 courthouse can be seen in the upper left corner of the picture. The courthouse is situated in a square. Pawnee has a population of 2,500 persons.

A view of the streets of Pawnee during the Kennamer trial

Court convenes at 9 AM. Dr. Karl A. Menninger of Topeka, Kansas, is recalled to the stand. He is given a review of Phil's life by Flint Moss and is asked the hypothetical question again, regarding whether Kennamer was insane when he killed John Gorrell.

"I think he was irrational and not fully aware of the circumstances."

When asked why, Dr. Menninger says, "I think he was unable to distinguish right from wrong because of his mental illness, and that illness is of such a nature that he was incapable of accepting ordinary standards and substituted his own. His own egotism was so great and his omnipotence was so great that he had his own moral code, such to him seemed a better one than the one which society accepts."

Dr. Menninger believes that Phil has a mental illness generally accepted as psychopathic personality. A psychopath is a person who cannot keep out of trouble, hardboiled men, habitual criminals. They do not lack intelligence, do not have illusions, but are eternal puzzles to the court. Menninger says that according to his definition of people with a perverted personality, they "are the lice of civilization."

He says Phil should get treatment but not in prison. "I wouldn't recommend the penitentiary. I don't think it cures persons of this type; it only cultivates their criminal tendencies."

At 11:20, Dr. E. A. Werner of Oklahoma City gives similar testimony. He, too, is a doctor of mental and nervous diseases and has worked for the United States Veteran's Administration for the last fourteen years. Dr. Werner testifies that he first examined Phil on January 12, 1935, for three and a half hours, then again the next day, and a third time a week later. When asked whether he thinks Phil could tell the difference between right and wrong the night of the murder, Dr. Werner states, "No, sir, I do not."

Dr. E. A. Werner

"Do you believe that on that night he understood, appreciated the consequences of his own act?"

"No, sir, I do not think so."

Prosecution attorney King briefly cross-examines Dr. Werner and asks if he agrees with Dr. Menninger.

"I do," replies Dr. Werner.

At 11:35, court is adjourned for lunch recess and will reconvene at 1 PM. Judge Hurst orders the courtroom to be cleared of spectators during the lunch recess, after learning that "several urchins" were going to occupy seats and sell them for $1 each. Many of the cafés report that they are sold out during the noon hour rush.

At 1:10 PM, Phil Kennamer is called to the stand. He's wearing a double-breasted blue serge suit with a gray buttoned-down collar shirt and a gray-and-white patterned necktie. His face is expressionless. He looks pale and tight-lipped but sits at ease on the witness stand. After being sworn in, he stares directly at Virginia Wilcox, while she appears impassive, sitting in the front row between her brother Homer and Opal Kennamer. Dr. and Mrs. Gorrell stare at Phil. He takes the stand for three hours and twenty minutes. Each answer he gives is deliberate and clipped, while the courtroom is silent. Spectators are breathless as they hang on every word.

Defense Attorney Charles B. Stuart

Defense attorney C. B. Stuart begins by questioning Phil about the details of how he came to meet John Gorrell, the trip to

Kansas City, the extortion note, his conversation with Floyd Huff, and the events of the night leading up to the murder. Stuart asks about Phil's meeting with Gorrell on Thanksgiving evening and how he came to shoot him. Phil is very succinct in answering each question. His mental clarity convinces the spectators and the jury that he is very sane, contrary to what his attorney wants to prove.

Attorney Stuart asks Phil about Ted Bath's testimony, when he said that Phil had suggested taking the compromising pictures of Virginia Wilcox and Barbara Boyle. Phil denies that he made such a suggestion about Virginia, enunciating each word of his answer, "I . . . did . . . not," very slowly.

About killing Gorrell: "I did what I did to save my own life."

About Virginia Wilcox: "I fell in love with Miss Wilcox when I first met her three years ago. I have loved her ever since and love her now," he says in a quiet voice.

About his motive for the killing: "My sole motive was to protect Virginia Wilcox from kidnapping."

Prosecuting attorney King bluntly begins his cross-examination. "Do you know right from wrong?"

"Yes, I think so," answers Phil.

"Have you always known right from wrong?"

"Yes."

"You're conscious of the fact that statements of certain witnesses [who] have testified are contradictory to yours?"

"Yes."

"You still think your answers were right?"

"Yes, I'm certain," declares Phil.

King asks Phil about the letter from Gorrell and making some "easy money": "You don't have it now?"

"No."

"That's the letter that formed your excuse for a visit to Kansas City?"

"I'd say it had everything to do with going to Kansas City."

"And it is not now in evidence?"

Moss objects to King's line of questioning, stating that it is an "unlawyer-like" method of cross-examining.

King asks about Phil's association with Booth, to whom he was introduced by some friends.

"Did you have occasion to visit Booth again?" asks King.

"Yes. To purchase some whisky."

When Phil is asked whether he ever discussed kidnaping Virginia Wilcox with Booth, he denies it.

"Didn't you notify Booth you were interested in big money and asked him if he wouldn't be interested in kidnaping some wealthy Tulsans and name Miss Wilcox?"

Moss objects to the question, probably on the grounds of badgering the witness, because King has asked the same question twice.

"Your witness says he wants to answer," says King.

"Well, be a lawyer!" shouts Moss.

The court overrules the objection, and Phil denies making the comment to Booth.

Then Dixie Gilmer and Charles Stuart get into a heated exchange when Gilmer hears him make a comment to his associates. Stuart shakes his finger at Gilmer. "Young man, don't interrupt me when I'm talking to my associates!"

Judge Hurst raps his gavel and says, "Let's get along."

When asked, Phil also denies meeting anyone at the airport in Kansas City when he and Gorrell try to rent a plane.

"Were there parachutes in the plane?" asks King.

"After the plane was refused, I remarked that I wouldn't go up on a day like that without a parachute."

King asks Phil if he had any communication with friends while he was in jail.

"No." Then Phil realizes he forgot about the coded notes that were passed and admits to them.

King, holding up a copy of the coded notes, asks if Phil was trying to locate the missing Gorrell letter. Phil says no. But King hands Phil the copy of the coded note that says otherwise. Phil reads it and comments that a word had been changed.

Moss stands and shouts, "That's not the way lawyers try lawsuits. It may be the way of politicians," and he objects to King's line of questioning.

Judge Hurst gives him a reprimand.

"Be merciful with him. He knows not what he does," retorts King. He, too, draws a reprimand from Judge Hurst.

Moss insists that the copy of the coded notes be admitted into evidence, and they are. King refers to the word *sweetheart* on the copy and asks Phil to explain.

"I'd like to explain that," Phil says. "I think it was an act of the *Tulsa World* to inject an element of eroticism in this case," getting in a jab at Lee.

King hands a copy of the decoded notes to Phil, who confirms the translation. King then passes this copy to the jury. A lull comes over the courtroom, as each member of the jury takes the time to read it, while Phil remains calmly seated.

After a few more questions to Phil, a recess is called. Phil steps down from the stand, confident and cocky. He puts his arm around Stuart's shoulder and whispers in his ear at the defense table.

When court reconvenes, King continues his cross-examination of Phil. "Phil, on Thanksgiving night you didn't have dinner at home?"

"I had, but not with my family. I was late."

"Had you been drinking?"

"Very little."

"When did you begin to drink to excess?"

"Oh. Two or three years ago."

King asks Phil about Sidney's death: Was it "merely a coincidence that Sidney Born was killed?"

"No, I never said that," Phil replies. "I said he was murdered. I know he didn't commit suicide. I think he was murdered—"

Stuart objects, and it's sustained.

King asks Phil about the night Sidney drove him to St. John's Hospital.

"When Sidney delivered you there, you saw Gorrell's car at the curb, the engine running and the right door open?"

"I'm not sure about the engine, but I don't think the door was open."

"You entered the car before John returned?"

"No."

"Isn't it a fact that you got the gun out of the pocket and had it in your possession when he returned?"

"No, Mr. King, that is not the truth."

Then King asks Phil to tell what happened that night.

"I got in the car from the right side. I am almost certain the door was closed. Gorrell was seated at the wheel. I think the first thing he said was 'I've been waiting twenty minutes.' I told him I was sorry, I had been delayed. The next conversation was of a trivial nature."

"You and John were intimate, were you not?"

"I had never known John very well. I noticed he was more reserved than usual. His conversation was desultory. Trivial, but not light."

"Any sign of nervousness on the part of either of you?"

"I couldn't say as to myself. Gorrell seemed morose, restrained, and not as cordial as usual."

"Who suggested the route to take on leaving the hospital?"

"No one made a suggestion."

"John Gorrell sought the scene of his own death?"

"He was at least driving in that direction," responds Phil.

"You and John were the only two in the car?" asks King.

"Yes."

"No struggle took place at the hospital or before the scene of the murder?"

"That's correct."

"Do you know if any one witnessed the struggle?"

"I'm morally certain no one did."

King then asks about pulling the trigger: "You are certain the gun had been snapped once or twice before it was fired?"

"I know it was snapped once, but my memories thereafter are incoherent."

"How long was it before the two shots were fired?

"One to two seconds."

After a few more questions, King ends his cross-examination. It's 4:10 PM.

King asks more questions of Phil and ends his cross-examination at 4:10.

Stuart has a re-direct examination of Phil on some points that were brought up during King's cross-examination and asks Phil about being a "habitual drunkard."

Phil states that he began drinking heavily two or three years earlier but denies that he is a "habitual drunkard" and says his drinking "was among his friends." He leaves the stand at 4:15, appearing very self-assured.

"The defense rests," announces Flint Moss.

How helpful was Phil's testimony? Did it help or hurt Moss's insanity defense? During his time on the stand, Phil appeared to be very sane and cognizant of his actions prior to the murder, contradicting statements many witnesses have testified to, thus chipping away at Moss's defense.

Court is adjourned at 4:30.

Tuesday, February 19

- Day 8 of the Trial — State Rebuttals -

Not as many spectators show up this morning when court convenes, and there is less excitement on the witness stand. Everett Gardner, Gorrell's roommate in Kansas City, has been here several days to be used as a rebuttal witness. Prosecution attorney Anderson does not believe Phil's insinuation that Gardner was "one of the boys" and has no intention of questioning him.

At 9 AM, the state begins its rebuttal testimony with **Jenkin Lloyd Jones**, a reporter at the *Tulsa Tribune*. It's in regard to a newspaper article written by Jones and a comment that Judge Kennamer made during the Machine Gun Kelly trial on September 21, 1933. Jones wanted to get a high official to comment on the federal action to crack down on gangsters, and Gilmer wants to read that article to the court.

Moss objects to the introduction of the article, saying, "What Judge Kennamer may have said about another person is not material."

"Overruled," replies Judge Hurst.

Moss asks Jones if he writes in shorthand.

"No," responds Jones.

"This article, you know, is not an actual quotation of Judge Kennamer," states Moss.

"It is not a verbatim account but my memory."

"You do not contend the article is an accurate reproduction of what he said?"

"No, it's not a verbatim account but expressed his views."

Judge Hurst then decides the newspaper clipping need not be introduced.

Gilmer asks Jones to recall the conversation he had with Judge Kennamer, but Moss again objects, and it's sustained.

"On September 21, 1933," begins Gilmer to Jones, "did he make this statement: 'Criminals—'"

"I object!" shouts Moss.

"Overruled."

Gilmer begins again. "Did he say, 'Criminals, of course, are just as individual as law-abiding citizens. There are fat criminals and lean criminals, strong criminals and weak criminals, and smart criminals and stupid criminals. But in my observations, extending over a number of years, I have come to the conclusion that most of them, the habitual type especially, have one trait in common, namely a strange quirk of the mind, which gives them an anti-social tendency. It is not strong enough to be classed as insanity, but it is akin to it.'"

Moss objects again, but the judge overrules it.

"Yes, that's what he said in substance," answers Jones.

"No cross examination," replies Moss. His numerous attempts to suppress the article and Jones's comments have further chipped away at his already weakened defense.

At 9:15 AM, Gilmer calls the next witness, **Vera Van Tassel**, who is the secretary to the Sand Springs school's superintendent. She brings Phil's intelligence and educational quotient records from the time when he attended the school, from 1924 to 1928. Moss objects to the admission of these records as evidence, because this information is dated and cannot be relevant to the case. The attorneys confer at the bench.

After the conference, Van Tassel is dismissed without testifying. Moss's objection stands, and he avoids another drubbing of his defense pleas.

At 9:20 AM, **Mossie Holmes,** from the Tulsa board of education, takes the stand. She is in charge of tests and measurements and has an educational test that Phil took called the Stanford Seaman test.

Moss objects to the admission of this record into evidence but is overruled.

She says, "On this particular time, this boy was fourteen years and four months old. His test revealed him to have the knowledge of eighteen years and eight months. He stood at the top of his class. The one next to him was a year below in achievement."

Again, Moss's efforts to suppress evidence of Phil's intelligence are thwarted, and this witness tears another hole in his insanity defense. She is dismissed.

At 9:30 AM, Dixie Gilmer calls to the stand **Gertrude Hart** of Tulsa, a secretary at Cascia Hall. She is in charge of scholastic records and produces test results from when Phil attended the school in September 1933. Phil had scored a 117 plus, compared to the normal rating of 100. Again, Moss objects to the admission of this record and is overruled once more. Trying to deflect another dagger to the defense team, Moss stands to read aloud a question from the test: "'Frank had twelve marbles and lost six. How many does he have left?' Now don't you think that is a simple question to ask an eighteen-year-old?"

Miss Hart attempts to answer, but Gilmer and Moss both work on keeping her quiet. Gilmer is hoping the judge will rule, and Moss is not finished with what he wants to say.

Gilmer points out that the question is one of many. "Tell them the whole thing." he addresses the witness.

"These tests have a time limit. This particular question is a standard recognized test over the United States," explains Hart.

Moss reads another question from the test. "'Why do we buys clocks? Because we like to hear them strike, because they have hands, because they tell time?'

"That's a sample of the other questions, is it?" he asks.

"Yes," replies Mrs. Hart.

Moss works hard to discredit the validity of Phil's test results, because the judge overruled his objection to admitting them.

She is dismissed.

At 9:40, **C. C. Jelks**, the director of Sand Springs vocational education, is called to the stand. He has been at the school for sixteen years. He testifies that Phil irregularly attended the school for five years, and, in his opinion, Phil knew the difference between right and wrong.

At 9:45 AM, next on the stand is **Dr. G. W. Robinson** of Kansas City. He has been a consultant for the Veteran's Bureau and was the superintendent of the state hospital for the insane of

Missouri. He has also done work in hospitals and sanitariums. Although Dr. Robinson has never met Phil, he was in court when the facts and observations about Phil were read on Monday.

Mr. King asks, "Keeping in mind those facts and the observation of the defendant on the stand, in your judgment was Kennamer, on the night of the tragedy, rational or irrational? Did he know right from wrong? Was he sane or insane, and is he now sane?"

"It is my opinion that at that time he was sane, rational, knew the consequences of his own act, and knew the difference between right and wrong."

In his cross-examination, Mr. Moss asks, "Isn't it extraordinary to pass an opinion such as this without a personal examination of the person on whose sanity you are passing?"

"We judge sanity or insanity by the individual's conduct and conversation. He didn't talk, look, or act like an insane man on the stand," answers the doctor.

"I insist on a direct answer."

"No. I'll have to explain my answer."

"I don't want an explanation," says a frustrated Moss.

Judge Hurst says that the doctor may explain.

"I'll withdrawal the question," says Moss. "What consideration in the deciding of a person's sanity or insanity do you give to an IQ test made ten years prior to the examination of the patient?"

"IQ tests are often unsatisfactory, and I wouldn't give much attention to that, if I was making an examination."

At 10:00 AM, **Dr. B. W. Griffin** is called to the stand. He is the medical superintendent of the Norman Insane Hospital. Mr. King addresses the witness's qualifications. The doctor has never met Phil and has not examined him but has heard Phil testify and is aware of the hypothetical question put to the previous witnesses.

"Basing your testimony on your personal observation, listening to the testimony, by observing him on the stand, in your judgment, was he rational or irrational, did he know right from wrong, was he sane or insane at the time of the tragedy?" asks Mr. King.

"I think he was sane at the time of the act and knew the consequences of his act," answers the doctor.

Mr. Moss cross-examines, "Now, is it your judgment that the defendant is a normal boy?"

"I think he is a psychopathic personality."

Mr. Moss asks for a definition of "psychopathic personality."

"My interpretation is he's a man who cannot take the standards of society for his rule. He has the brain power, has the intellect, but he is a man who can be an intellectual giant but a moral weakling. He does not have the same standards, the same value of life and property that normal people do have. He is not insane, but he is up to that level."

"He needs treatment, doesn't he, in order to correctly value life, property, and the customs of society, doesn't he?" asks Mr. Moss.

"We haven't a place for such people where, over a period of years, we can correct them. I believe Judge Kennamer has had trouble all the way through. I think Phil has been put off by his friends, and he became desperate."

"In that desperation, with these abnormalities, then when he came to the point where you say he was put off by his friends, didn't that make him mentally sick?"

"It made him more desperate. He's not mentally sick."

"He's inadequate, not mentally sick. It made him more mentally inadequate, didn't it?"

"He has an inferiority complex and fought against it to prove he was a man. I think that is the reason he killed John Gorrell."

"All of these psychopathic personalities drink to console themselves?" asks Mr. Moss.

"No. They can't control themselves."

"He can't control it, in your judgment?"

"I think not."

"You say such a man who can't control himself isn't insane?"

"Not to my way."

"Does a psychopathic personality with an increasing desperation, drinking to cheer himself, ever go so far in the progress of the disease they don't know right from wrong?"

"It is possible."

"He's already departed from his psychopathic state, hasn't he?"

"He's just like a lot of people in the country who go to make our crimes. Legally, I say he's sane."

Mr. King asks whether Phil could be cured if he were sent to the Norman Institution.

Mr. Moss objects and is overruled.

"I don't think we're equipped to give him the type of treatment he should have. I think you can only raise him to a certain level and hope."

"Isn't it a fact that Granite and other penitentiaries have many psychopathic personalities?"

Mr. Moss's objection is sustained.

"There are institutions in the country where the patient could receive treatment?" asks Mr. King.

"Not sure, but there is a government institution at El Reno that is equipped to take care of him."

At 10:20 AM, **Dr. Felix N. Adams**, superintendent of the Vinita State Insane Hospital, is called to the stand. His professional specialty has been with mental diseases since 1909, and he has worked at the hospital since 1912. He has also been in the courtroom and has heard Phil's testimony and the hypothetical question that was posed to the other doctors.

Mr. King asks, "Do you agree he is a psychotic personality?"

"I do," says Dr. Adams.

"So you believe he knew right from wrong and the consequences of his act when he killed John Gorrell."

"I think he knew right from wrong."

"Do you think he is sane or insane?"

"Sane."

"Do you think he is a psychopathic personality without psychosis?"

"I do."

"And is it true, is it not, that the psychosis is the determining point in insanity?"

"It is."

"Do you believe the defendant would respond to treatment in your institution?"

"He wouldn't respond to treatment."

During the cross-examination, the doctor states that people like Phil do not respond to home training, and that they will be above average in some subjects at school.

"As they advance in school and age, they are hard to control and cause both parents and authorities trouble," says Dr. Adams. "After they leave school, they are restless. They move from one position to another. They usually go through life that way. Some go on and make respectable citizens, but the large majority of them are the distinct antisocial type."

"What is your definition for insanity?" asks Mr. Moss.

"There are several forms of the disease in the mind and different degrees."

"To any extent, is this defendant insane?"

"I wouldn't say so," the doctor replies.

"Do psychopathic personalities ever become legally insane?"

"Legally and medically insane."

"Is this boy medically insane?'

"No, I don't think so, because he has never developed a psychosis."

"What is psychosis?" asks Mr. Moss.

"Hallucinations, periods of depression—feeble-minded persons, epileptics develop it. It means simply insanity."

"He needs treatment?"

"Yes," replies the doctor.

Mr. King asks Dr. Adams, "After all is said, you say he was sane on the night of the tragedy and is sane now?"

Moss objects, and Judge Hurst says, "I think that is repetition."

Hanley "Cadillac" Booth
(courtesy of Gateway to Oklahoma History)

At 10:55 AM, Mr. King calls **Hanley "Cadillac" Booth** of Oklahoma City to the stand. Booth, who had to be subpoenaed to testify, says that he first met Phil in July of 1934, then again in August when Phil came to purchase whisky from him, which was his business at the time. He is now in the bond business, and his office is located next door to the police station.

Mr. King asks, "Did you and Phil have a conversation to [sic—about] hijacking and extortion at that time?"

Mr. Moss objects, and both he and Mr. Gilmer confer at the bench. Mr. King and Mr. Wallace join them. The judge sustains the objection.

Mr. Moss cross-examines and asks, "Did Phil Kennamer at that time discuss with you extortion, kidnap, or robbery or some Tulsa people and, at the time, tell you about the Wilcox girl?"

"Yes."

"Did you think he was crazy or not?" asks Mr. Moss.

Gilmer objects, and Judge Hurst sustains it.

"Did you think he was serious or not?"

"I couldn't tell. I didn't pay any attention to him."

"Why didn't you pay attention?"

"It didn't mean anything to me."

"How many times have you been convicted?" Mr. Moss quickly asks.

"About a hundred times. I pleaded guilty. Paid one fine to the government, served thirty days on conviction in federal court."

Booth has been a bootlegger for years, transporting and selling alcohol during these times of Prohibition, and has probably lost count of how many times he has actually been arrested.

At 11:05 AM, **Mr. Harry Carmichael,** a former Tulsa school principal at Horace Mann School and currently a superintendent for Perry public schools, is called to the stand. Mr. King attempts to ask about John Gorrell's character and his years as a student, but Mr. Moss repeatedly objects to the line of questioning. Is it relevant to bring up how good or bad John Gorrell was as a student? Or was it out of fear that this witness could inflict more damage to his insanity defense? But the state insists on asking the witness about Gorrell as a student. The attorneys quietly confer with the judge at the bench.

Court is suddenly recessed for lunch, and Carmichael is never recalled as a witness.

Since the Pawnee restaurants are so busy during the lunch recess, many people bring their lunch, including Virginia Wilcox and Geraldine Snedden, Jack Snedden's mother. They sit side by side in the front row, so that they won't lose their seats when court reconvenes.

At 1:05 PM, Tulsa police detective **L. D. Kern** is called to the stand in place of Mr. Carmichael. Detective Kern was assigned to investigate the Gorrell case on the night of the murder.

Mr. Lee Johnson, of the prosecution, asks, "Did you, in the progress of your investigation, make an investigation into the character of John Gorrell?"

Moss objects, and the objection is sustained.

"Do you know his reputation as a peaceful, law-abiding citizen in Tulsa?"

Mr. Moss objects again, and it is sustained.

Mr. Johnson has a point to prove and needs to discuss it with the judge. Judge Hurst excuses the jury, while he and Johnson confer at the bench. Johnson wants to show that that in a prior criminal court of appeals case in August 1930, a defendant killed a man while he was drunk, and the state showed the good reputation of the deceased. The rule is that when the defense attacks the reputation of the deceased, then the state will offer proof as to the character of the deceased. Johnson wants to prove that because Phil knew that Gorrell was plotting to kidnap Virginia, in theory Gorrell should have been killed as an act of glory because Gorrell was trying to violate the law. The defense argues its point that this is not relevant, because it never offered any testimony that Gorrell was a dangerous character and asks what purpose would it serve? The defense wins its point, and Dr. Kern is dismissed from the stand.

At 1:30 PM, **Otto Kramer,** who is a friend to both Kennamer and Gorrell, is called to the stand. The twenty-one-year-old has known Phil for four years but has become closer to him in the last two or three years.

Mr. Gilmer asks, "Have you ever had any conversation with Kennamer when the name of Virginia Wilcox was injected?"

"Yes."

"On one occasion or more?"

"Several."

"Was the substance of these conversations about the same?"

"They amounted to pretty much the same, very little variation."

"State the substance of the conversations."

"I'd have to refer to a few facts that it is evident were involved—"

"I object!" says Moss. He doesn't want this witness's "facts" introduced, because they could be construed as an opinion or hearsay.

"It appears—" continues Kramer.

"I object!" Moss says again, .

Judge Hurst sustains the objection, agreeing with the defense that the witness should not inject what could be his opinion but should simply state the facts as he himself has seen or heard them.

"He stated he was very fond of Miss Wilcox at one time, and she didn't care for his attentions, and he felt very bitterly toward her and her family and said he was going to get even, if it took him to his last day," says Kramer.

"That is all," says Gilmer, and Kramer is dismissed. Moss does not cross-examine the witness. But why not? Kramer has just testified that Phil said he would seek revenge on Virginia for his unrequited love. Was Phil really that angry with Virginia and her family? Moss thinks not and that Kramer's testimony is just an aberration to testimony already introduced, all of it pointing to Phil's undying love for Virginia.

At 1:42 PM, Mr. Gilmer calls to the stand **Dr. C. C. Knoblock**, a chemist from Tulsa who operates a laboratory. Gilmer shows the doctor a photo of the head of John Gorrell revealing the two bullet holes. He is asked about which of the two holes came from the first shot and what interval of time elapsed between the first and second shots.

"The one in the interior part of the forehead was fired first," says the doctor, pointing to the bullet wound toward the front in the photo.

"Can you say what interval of time elapsed, if any, between the two shots?"

Mr. Moss objects, and the objection is overruled. He knows that the answer could lead the jury to believe that the second shot was intentional, not in self-defense.

Dr. Knoblock continues to answer: "The normal clotting time of blood is four to five minutes. The outside temperature doesn't have a great deal of effect on blood. Taking all things into consideration, the fact that the blood of the second wound has flowed over the face, as well as the first, I think it is fair to say the first blood would coagulate in a minute and a half. The blood from the first wound flowed down and of necessity was clotted before the second wound was inflicted."

"What is the minimum amount of time that you think elapsed between the firing of the two shots?" asks Gilmer.

"There can be no denying that there was an interval, because there was a crossing of the two paths of blood. Considering the facts that cause blood to coagulate, there would have to be at least a minute."

Phil said that the shots happened quickly, within seconds. Now a specialist has contradicted Phil's testimony and delivers another blow to the defense team. Why did it take Phil another minute to fire the second shot? Was it for good measure to make sure John was dead? Or was it that Phil pulled the trigger again, thinking the first shot went astray? Regardless, the self-defense plea has been damaged. If there had been a struggle for the gun, the first shot should have stopped the wrestling match.

Mr. Moss cross-examines the doctor in an effort to change the witness's testimony. "What was the time that elapsed between the taking of the photograph and the finding of the body?" asks Moss.

The state objects to the question and is sustained.

Moss wants to contend that because photos of John's head wounds were taken at different times, there could be an error in the doctor's testimony about the coagulation of the blood. "Was there any appreciable difference in looking at the photographs in the time at which they were made?"

"I wouldn't like to qualify on that. These are entirely different pictures," comments the doctor.

"Sure, they are," says Moss, "There is more blood in [exhibit] seven than [exhibit] six, is there not?"

"Well, one is an enlargement." Then Doctor Knoblock takes out a pencil and paper to make some calculations regarding the pictures.

"Let us assume these two wounds were inflicted around twelve o'clock, and within thirty or forty-five minutes that the body was removed from the Titus home to a downtown undertaker's. Would there be more blood flow in that movement?"

"The serum, a clear fluid, might flow."

This cross-examination is not going in Moss's favor, and he becomes frustrated. He asks more provoking questions, and a verbal sparring ensues. After a few minutes, Moss finishes his unsuccessful attempts to trip up the witness, and Dr. Knoblock is dismissed.

At 1:59 PM, Mr. Anderson announces that the state rests. Mr. Moss says that the defense also rests. Judge Hurst calls for a recess to prepare instructions for the jury.

There were twenty-six witnesses who testified for the state and thirteen for the defense.

Late in the afternoon, at 4:10 PM, after a two-hour conference with counsel, Judge Hurst delivers his instructions to the jurors. They must make a decision of:

1. Murder, with life imprisonment or the death penalty to be fixed by the jury.
2. Manslaughter in the first degree, with confinement in prison of not less than four years, to be fixed by the jury or left to the court.
3. Acquittal on the grounds of insanity at the time of the commission of the offense; or
4. Acquittal on the plea of self-defense.

Judge Hurst takes fifteen minutes to read the instructions:

Homicide is manslaughter in the first degree when perpetrated without a design to effect death and in a heat of passion, but in a cruel manner, unless committed under circumstances as to constitute excusable or justifiable homicide. There is no evidence tending to show that the homicide in this case was excusable. The defendant has interposed as one of his defenses the plea of insanity.

In this connection, you are instructed that under the law of this state, an act done by a person in a state of insanity cannot be punished as a public offense, and the following persons are incapable of committing crimes: lunatics, insane persons, and all persons of unsound minds, including persons temporarily or partially deprived of reason, upon proof that at the time of committing the act charged against them they were incapable of knowing its wrongfulness.

The law presumes every person to be sane and able to distinguish right from wrong as applied to any particular act, and to understand the nature and consequences of such act, until a reasonable doubt of his sanity is raised by competent evidence. The burden of this insanity proof is on the defendant. It is sufficient if he raises in the minds of the jury only a reasonable doubt as to his sanity.

If you believe at the time he fired the shot that took the life of Gorrell, that he knew right from wrong, you would not be justified in acquitting him by reason of insanity.

If you do entertain a reasonable doubt as to his sanity, it is your duty to resolve that doubt in his favor and acquit him.

On the self-defense theory, the court instructed the jury to determine if the facts justified the defendant in thinking his life was in danger at the time the shots were fired. You are instructed when one is unlawfully attacked, he has the right to use such force as appears necessary, if he uses greater force than is necessary then he is guilty of manslaughter.

If you find the defendant was the aggressor and sought the deceased and provoked the difficulty, he cannot plead self-defense and should be convicted of murder.

If he sought the defendant and provoked the difficulty without intending to kill him or inflict serious injury, he would be guilty of manslaughter.

If you find that the defendant sought the deceased for the purpose of dissuading the deceased from carrying out his threatened plan to kidnap Virginia Wilcox or extort money from her father, and did not engage in or provoke a difficulty, then the defendant is entitled to avail himself on the plea of self-defense.

If the deceased were making a demonstration with the gun, which led the defendant to believe he was in danger of his life, he would be justified on the grounds of self-defense, unless he was the aggressor.

Even if John Gorrell planned to kidnap Virginia Wilcox, the defendant had no right to kill him to prevent the plan being carried out. If you believe he killed Gorrell with a premeditated design, then you should convict him of murder.

Court is recessed at 4:27 PM until 9 AM tomorrow.

Wednesday, February 20

- Day 9 of the Trial — Defense Rebuttals -

At 9 AM, Prosecutor **Tom Wallace** begins his fiery rebuttal. He asks the jury to find Phil Kennamer guilty of murder and demands the death penalty. "There's no manslaughter in this case," he declares. "The facts warrant a death penalty, but I'm not the one to ask the death of a man. That is for you to judge." Wallace says that it's clear to him what happened. He believes Kennamer got to the hospital first, found Gorrell's car with the pistol in the door pocket, and made Gorrell drive to Forest Boulevard and deliberately killed him. The motive was to prevent exposure of Phil's part in the extortion plot. He also pointed out that Phil made threats to kill Gorrell to other members of the High-Hat Club, but Floyd Huff was the only person who went to the police and told them, after he'd heard Gorrell had been killed. "Did any of Kennamer's young friends do that? They did not."

TOM WALLACE
Prosecuting Attorney

Wallace attacks the defense of Phil's insanity: "He was wise enough not to kill Gorrell in Kansas City, where he didn't have Flint Moss to help him and where his father wasn't a federal judge!" he shouts. "No, no. That boy's not insane. He's smart. He thinks he can outsmart this jury." He also tells the jury that they should judge Phil Kennamer without regard to the fact that his father is a federal judge.

"I sympathize with his father. I know he is trying to save his boy, but what is going to take place at the end of the road is what you men are going to do. Many boys have been unmanageable, but they didn't become criminals.

"And then coming back from a party one night, he jumped from one car to another. They will tell you that is a scene of insanity. You take and run two cars side by side, forty to sixty miles an hour, going at the same speed. All you do is step from one running board to another. There's no art in that at all. You've done it. So have I. Any normal boy does those crazy stunts. Nothing abnormal about that.

Mrs. Gorrell sits quietly in the courtroom as Wallace begins his closing remarks. She begins to weep after an hour and sobs heavily when Wallace picks up the gun that killed her son. Mr. Gorrell nervously chews his unlit cigar.

Wallace, during his appeal, would raise his voice and clap his hands together to make a point. At other times, his voice would fall to a whisper.

"He [Phil] said he had an engagement with Gorrell at the hospital that night. I'll tell you what happened. Phil saw that Gorrell was in the car. Phil said he was. He's too smart to admit he wasn't and tell you why. The girl said the pistol was sticking up in the pocket and Phil said he knew the car. I think Phil went to the car and saw the pistol while John was going up to the door [of the hospital] . . . He says John was sitting in the car. I just don't believe it.

"A doctor has told you that a minute elapsed between two shots. Then they [the defense] tell you, Phil Kennamer tells you, 'we got in a scuffle and the gun went off.' You just know that's not the truth. There's not a wrinkle in the coat, not a hair mussed up. Look at the photograph. No struggle took place there," says Wallace.

"There is nothing to this self-defense story. He said he was going to kill Gorrell, and he did it. It's up to you now as the sole judges. We've proven John Gorrell is dead, that Kennamer said he'd kill him, that he did kill him, and I'm satisfied you believe that Kennamer knew right from wrong when he did it. Young Kennamer wouldn't say he shot Gorrell without an excuse. You have a spoiled boy, a cold-blooded boy to deal with. You said you'd convict him of murder if the facts warranted it. You can say we find the defendant guilty and fix the punishment at death, or you can send him to prison for life. If you think it is justified, you can return a manslaughter verdict. In my judgment, there's no manslaughter in this case. Let the law speak under the facts in the case. May He who walked on the sea guide you men in this case. Let's not be fooled by a glove, which fits both hands. Keep it on the hand with the punch in it."

Wallace concludes his argument after an hour and forty minutes, and court is recessed for a short break.

At 10:55 AM, **A. Flint Moss**, the suave and elegant lead defense attorney, is next. He makes references to what he calls Phil's insanity. His audience is serious, and so is Phil, who also looks tired and worried. "Has anyone told you this boy is normal?" demands Moss. "No, not one, except Phil. He thinks he's the smartest man in the courtroom, yes, indeed. That itself is a symptom of his mentality."

Virginia Wilcox is in the crowd, listening to Moss with her chin in her hands and watching Moss pace back and forth in front of the jury box. He taps one juror on the knee and waves his finger in the face of another.

Moss attacks the state's witness, Floyd Huff, to discredit his testimony, calling him "a deserter in the time of war, a spoiler of womanhood, and a common thief. That's what he is.

"The fact is real that John Gorrell was actively concerned in this conspiracy. You know," says Moss, as he wipes his brow, "I said that to a human mind comes a composite result of all our thoughts that makes us either good or bad, as we have lived. It illustrates the complete abandonment through the life of Gorrell. He ate dinner at his home, then he went to a friend's house where his parents were. He took this Word girl there for a while." Moss next takes aim at Gorrell's questionable character. "Then he went from that respectable home to a tourist camp with her. No, no, gentlemen. It's a tragic thing, but it's true. These things which have been presented make of poor John Gorrell a tragic sort of figure."

"When Virginia was in Michigan, Phil persuaded Jack Snedden to call her and say if she didn't write Phil a letter, he would drink himself to death. Did you ever do a stunt like that? No, you were never that deeply in love. That's abnormal. That's insane. Virginia did the sensible thing. She wouldn't write. Then Phil did another fantastic thing. He wrote Virginia, saying he had been drunk and Jack had only called her as a friendly act to him. He said he'd gotten over his drunk and love, but he gave it to Virginia's sweetheart that he was trying to cut out to mail. Did you ever do that? No. No man ever became so profoundly in love that he wrote a letter to his sweetheart and gave it to his rival to read and mail. You never heard of a boy doing that, did you?

"Was Phil's love dead?" continues Moss. "Did he seek only to remain Virginia's friend? No-o-o! Virginia says, down to the date of the tragedy, his effort to win her love continued unabated. Why, listen. In November, Phil did this. Snedden had a date with Virginia. Phil took Jack to the flower shop where he, Phil, bought the flowers and sent them to her without a card. Personally, I think she's more beautiful than the flowers. Love ranted in his breath for her, notwithstanding that she spurned his love. Did you ever do that?

"There's no dispute in this record, but the fact is—and you should treat it as a fact—Phil Kennamer's infatuation for her was alive, undimmed, down to the date of the tragedy. If that's the truth, Ted Bath is a liar. The same thing is true with that Kramer boy what he says. Phil told him last July or August that Virginia didn't love him, and he was going to get even with her. It can't be true.

"Bath says Kennamer threatened to kidnap her. If Phil loved her, Bath lied. Now then, may we treat it now, please, that this is at least an uncommon and extraordinary love Phil had for Virginia. Did he ever have any purpose for kidnaping her? On October 12, he told her brother Gorrell has this plan to kidnap her. Before Phil told her brother, he told Jack Snedden, Virginia's sweetheart and her lover, that Gorrell intended to kidnap her. Could he have selected a better method to communicate it to her?

"It is uncontradicted that before the middle of October, Phil Kennamer had notified both of the Wilcox children John Gorrell intended to kidnap Virginia.

"Doesn't it seem absurd for any lawyer to say he intended to kidnap her? Gorrell is the man who conceived the kidnaping scheme. Gorrell put it forward. Gorrell kept it alive. Phil's alarm made him go to Kansas City and get indisputable evidence that John Gorrell intended to go through with it.

"Here's John Gorrell, who, by everything he's done and said, proposes to go through with it, and Kennamer says he won't let him. Who would start that fight? Who was right or wrong? Isn't it right, laudable, and lawful to interrupt a kidnapping scheme? Phil Kennamer had that purpose. Would you refuse to give him that credit you'd demand for yourself? Phil had a right, it was his duty as a citizen, to tell Gorrell anything that would stop the plot. That's the law. If Gorrell started to pull the gun, Phil Kennamer had a right to do his derndest to prevent being harmed.

"Phil says the shots were fired in quick succession. Then we have an expert. God bless these experts. He told you from the photographs that a minute elapsed between the shots. He told you the two photos were taken at the same time.

"H. B. Maddux had already told you the two were taken a mile and a half apart. Are you going to believe that kind of expert?

"The burden and obligation is upon the state to prove beyond the shadow of a reasonable doubt that he was responsible. Have they done it?

"I agree when upon the street of Chicago brave young men surrounded John Dillinger and gave him less than half a chance. I agree with Governor Rolf of California when last summer they caught two kidnappers and lynched them publicly, and he said 'I want kidnapers disposed of that way.' I glorify the unremitting research that brought vicious Bruno Hauptmann to the bar and condemned him to death. I want the day to come when kidnappers can't exist in the nation. If I see aright, everyone who has followed this case knows that if Phil Kennamer is freed, we have arrived at another story in stopping kidnapping."

Moss concludes his impassioned oratory after one hour and thirty-nine minutes, and court is recessed for lunch.

At 1:30 PM, **J. Berry King**, former attorney general and now special prosecutor, addresses the court. "It has been a genuine pleasure, if one can sense a pleasure out of a tragedy of this kind, to try this case before your fine judge. I wish I could join with Flint Moss in promising my political support, but I cannot. If I lived in your district, I would join in pledging you my support. You have conducted this case in a manner that has been satisfactory to the state's side of the table and I am sure to the defense side. I congratulate you upon the way in which you tried the case. I congratulate the citizens of Pawnee County that you have afforded the opportunity to try this lawsuit in such as courtroom as this. I have studied the faces of you twelve men, and if you are not honest and if are not intelligent, then you cannot expect to find a jury of honest and intelligent men in Oklahoma.

"That is not flattery. It comes from the depths of my heart. I don't care what your verdict is in this case. I shall be satisfied with it, and I am sure the state of Oklahoma will be satisfied with it. I cannot pass this spot without congratulating the plowboy who came up from the farm and who has conducted his share of this case so well [referring to Dixie Gilmer]. Perhaps some day he may make it with Flint Moss as a criminal lawyer. Mr. Anderson may sometime achieve that place of prominence that Judge Stewart now holds. Akin to the entire bar of Oklahoma."

During his closing argument, King says he does not want Phil to get the death penalty, but rather wants to confine him "to halt his mad career of crime." He scornfully and sarcastically ridicules the idea that Phil is insane and tells the court that Flint Moss carries an insanity plea in his vest pocket.

In his characteristic pose of putting his hands in his pockets, King says, "I am asking the state of Oklahoma to do what the family has failed to do, check this boy in his career in crime." He talks loudly, pacing back and forth in front of the jury, shouting at times and pounding the rail on the jury box. "You have been told by His Honor that you must try this case by the law and the evidence. You are instructed that homicide is the killing of one human being by another and is murder when perpetrated without law and by premeditative design. That is the charge . . . murder."

King addresses the insanity plea of the defense and says that he has proved from his witnesses' testimony that Phil knows right from wrong, that he may be odd, but Phil is sane. "Insanity? Why, all the doctors agree he ought to be confined. So do I, personally. I don't wish to see my friend Judge Kennamer's son electrocuted. But I want him confined to where he'll be safe the rest of his life."

"If he's insane and you discharge him, you gentlemen had better hunt a psychiatrist and be examined yourself before you go home.

"The defendant would have you believe he was seriously in love with Virginia Wilcox. I think he had a dual personality and avaricious to get her father's millions. I believe Phil Kennamer concocted the kidnap scheme.

"I think it piqued Phil's pride because he couldn't gain Virginia's affections. After he tried everything, he felt he'd make himself a hero and save her from a kidnapping. So, still planning his defense, he told Jack Snedden he was going to Kansas City to kill John Gorrell, and that was before the note was ever written. Dr. Gorrell admitted it is in John's handwriting. The note was put in an envelope addressed to H. F. Wilcox. Gorrell didn't even know Miss Virginia. Kennamer knew the address."

As for the extortion note, King says, "Why didn't he mail the letter from Kansas City? The son of a federal judge, he knew the penalty of using the mails for such a purpose. . . . If Kennamer had been found with that note in his pocket, he was found to be an accomplice in this kidnapping plot, he would be today where Huff was—in the Alcatraz prison.

"He told Homer Jr. about the plot because he thought Homer would tell Virginia, and she would call him back to her, so he could fasten his love on her and his fist on her father's fortune. Why didn't he tell his own father of the plot? Certainly, he's the one man who should have been told."

King takes a sip of water and continues, "What do we find Phil doing with the extortion note? He showed it to his friends. I imagine he thought he could put the kidnapping through and then he could come dashing up on a white horse, free the girl, have her fall in his arms, and they'd be married and live happily ever afterwards." This draws laughter from the audience. "He may have thought he could scare Mr. Wilcox. He doesn't know him like I do. He was out to get some of his money. He planned to get $50,000 from the Wilcox Oil and Gas Company by an advertising scheme that petered out. So then he decided to try for $20,000 with the extortion note. There's the motive."

The attorney says he has his own theory about what happened on the night of the murder. According to the waitress, Miss Hafford, Sidney and Phil left about 11 PM and drove a mile and a half in seven minutes, at the High-Hat rate of speed, to meet Gorrell at the hospital. "Moss would have you believe Kennamer met Gorrell a block and a half away from the hospital door. He left the car door open. The pistol was in the pocket of the door. I believe Phil came out with Born and recognized the car and got out. Kennamer must have gotten in the car, and, seeing the pistol, he decided to kill Gorrell with his own gun. I think he had the gun in his hand when Gorrell came out and ordered him to drive away. There's only four beings in the world who could have known when they met: One is God, and the others are Kennamer, Gorrell, and Sidney Born.

"We don't know the conversation between Kennamer and Gorrell; Kennamer has told his story. Gorrell can't tell his. I believe whatever the conversation was had, Kennamer had the gun in his hand at the time. With the same deliberation he used in running away from home and school, he pulled the gun, shot Gorrell, struck the wounded youth, stepped back, viewed the body, and then, in a brutal manner, fired a second shot into the lifeless body, then walked away and bragged about it."

Displaying the photo of Gorrell's body in the car to the jury, King attacks the defense argument: "This photograph is the complete answer of his self-defense. When you have retired to your own jury chamber and consider this, when you see the form of that boy as that picture reflects it, and as it was in its natural condition at the time Phil Kennamer left it, you can't conceive of the idea that there had been any struggle. The testimony is that John Gorrell was 6 feet, 2 inches tall, and weighed 160 pounds, a giant beside this defendant, and if there had been a struggle, the big man would have had the advantage. At least, there would have been some disturbance of his body, some dislocation of his clothes. He sits there in cool death just as he rode with Phil Kennamer to that fatal spot."

Some of the jurors glance down as King displays the picture, while others look but continue to absorb the attorney's words.

"An able counsel will follow me with the finest statement ever made in Oklahoma. My friend Judge Stuart will cry, and he has been well paid for every tear that he sheds. I am like John Gorrell. My lips are sealed and whatever is said, I can't defend myself. The state of Oklahoma has had experts here who have no interest nor prejudice in the cause of justice. When you have gone to decide his guilt or innocence, I hope you will cast your vote so that you can go home and say you have tried to do what was right from your observations. And when you go to bed at night, you won't be afraid to go to sleep and you can say to the state of which you are a part, I have done my duty and the state will be satisfied."

After addressing the court for two hours and seven minutes, King concludes his monologue, and court is recessed for a short break.

At 3:40 PM, the bespectacled defense attorney **James A. McCollum** begins his dramatic rebuttal to, and attack on, King in an aggravated tone of voice: "Gentleman of the jury, I feel as if this building should be reconsecrated to the cause of justice. Have I been in the presence of a jury trial? Do my ears deceive me when

I think I've heard the content of that last presentation on behalf of the state? I thought, and still do, that this jury is a body constituted under the law of twelve men, impartial, owing the state no more than the defense. In twenty-five years, today is the first time I heard any lawyer say that the jury is on their side of the table, helping to prosecute.

"You men have had extensive jury service. I have never heard so solemn an occasion turned into a political convention. King nominated Anderson for political advancement at a trial where human blood has been spilled. I say, gentlemen, may we reconsecrate this building in the cause of justice?"

McCallum vents his frustration that during King's rebuttal, King nominated Holly Anderson, King's assistant, for political advancement and that Anderson is using this trial as "a political stepping-stone." McCallum seems to be twisting King's words, because King has not mentioned Anderson for any political office during the trial. Holly Anderson has made it known in the past that he has political aspirations. Yet it would appear that McCallum wants to use this as a diversion and cast the prosecution in a negative light, in an effort to bolster his client's case to the jury.

Getting back to his rebuttal, McCallum addresses what the state called Phil's "criminal career": "Gentlemen of the jury, they say there is a long criminal career, vicious, hard, experienced criminal this Phil Kennamer. What is the record? Has he ever been convicted? Did a single witness ever connect Phil Kennamer with any wrongdoing, save and except this particular transaction? Why pour to extreme all this poison into the argument against this boy? Analyze your thought and check the evidence and see if anyone is justified in saying he had a long criminal career? I'm not saying Phil is what we term a Sunday school boy. It is just as clear as day to me what has happened.

"This may help you to see the picture as it exists. You heard the testimony of Phil's particular mental condition. I don't know anything about mental diseases. When a man is a raving maniac, I can tell it, and that's just about all. I think you and everybody else not only believes but knows that Phil has a mental disorder of some kind. Two of the three authorities say he has legal insanity. Two or three say he doesn't.

"They say he is mentally deficient and needs treatment. I'm asking you if you know if he's legally insane or not. I'm honest with you, I don't. Do you know? If you do—fortunate. If you don't, you can't guess at it. You must follow the court's instructions and not guess away a human life but give him the benefit of the doubt. That's the boy we're dealing with—sane or insane.

"The evidence is that the father is not only busy at home but must leave home to hold court elsewhere. The boy's mother is bedfast. I'm saying that such characters as Huff, 'Cadillac'—the woods is full of them—find it easy to pick up the unguarded boy or girl and lead them astray. That's what happened to Phil. If a model father or mother has a wayward son or daughter, every wagging tongue starts wagging. They keep admitting the Judge Kennamer is a model father—but remember, he enforces the law.

"I want the county attorney to answer something else. Tell this jury the motive the state claims Kennamer had to kill John Gorrell. It's not natural to kill. There's a motive. One says it was in trying to attract Virginia's attention. Another says to get her father's money and then they say Kennamer had a desire to get a vicious revenge on the Wilcox family. You just can't have a murder without a motive. I want the county attorney to point in the record what indicates to him this wild conclusion that Phil got in the car before John. It's not in the record; they're not entitled to argue it. If he doesn't know that, he's just guessing. The state just can't accept the right theory, and they don't have it. The correct explanation drives them to our position and they know it.

"They qualified you on the death penalty, which meant to say we are going to use you to send this boy to the electric chair," says McCallum, addressing the jury. "Their own witnesses say he should be treated. To say the best medical experts on both sides say this boy is in such a mental condition he needs medical treatment, but the law has not provided such an institution, then you should do the only thing left for you to do and send him to the penitentiary. I would rather have a man ask me to commit murder than ask me to send a helpless, mentally deficient boy to the state penitentiary. That is an awful thing to think about, much less suggest. Send this boy to the penitentiary among hard, heartless characters because you have no other place to send him? There is ample law in Oklahoma to take care of him.

"Take this case, gentlemen. Don't be swept off your feet. It is just an ordinary lawsuit, like we have tried from time to time in this courtroom. They prove he was armed. They prove the motive.

They prove the self-defense. Gentlemen, I think I have said all I can say about all I can do to help you. If not, I apologize for holding you here so long."

McCallum takes his seat, after speaking for forty minutes.

At 4:20 PM, the state prosecutor, **Prentiss Rowe**, a heavy-set, middle-aged man with the tenacious stare of a bulldog, stands and faces the jury. "Gentlemen, life is full of tragedies. It is hard to explain and always leaves in its wake an innocent to suffer, and so it is in this case. I want to apologize for the physical condition I am in. When in church, I seem to have contracted the flu. I am hardly able to address you at this time. I hope you will bear with me.

Prentiss Rowe.

State prosecutor Prentiss Rowe

"I think, gentlemen of the jury, I can approach this argument as it should be approached, fairly and impartially, without prejudice in my heart and without desire to do anything that might be unfair or unjust to the defendant on trial in this case.

I do not conceive it to be the duty of a lawyer to attempt to misstate the facts or mislead the jury. After all, the one thing that concerns this jury and his honor on the bench and the people of the state is that truth shall prevail and that your verdict shall speak the truth dealing fairly with the people of the state of Oklahoma and the defendant in this case. There is no desire to inflict unnecessary feeling on the father in this case whose mouth is stilled at this time. There is no desire on my part to say an unkind word that would cause Judge Kennamer's heart to ache more than it does now. He has my sincere sympathy in this hour of his trial. I would not use his position or refer to it in any way that might influence this jury. . . .

"There is but one issue before you, and that is whether or not defendant on trial here is guilty of the crime charged. Stripping this case of all camouflage, the issue is simple and soon will be placed in your hands to decide whether or not this defendant should be found guilty at your hands or be acquitted.

"I believe that at this moment we can agree on some of the physical facts proved. There is no doubt that John Gorrell was killed on Thanksgiving Day in the city of Tulsa. That fact is established and admitted. There is no doubt, gentlemen of the jury, but that the defendant, Phil Kennamer, admitted the killing. That fact is therefore is established. The state contends that Kennamer killed Gorrell with a premeditated design to take his life, that he made threats to do the thing he did do. That fact is not disputed in this case. The testimony, however, from disinterested witnesses on that point is that Kennamer, before he went to Kansas City and on different occasions, stated that he intended to kill John Gorrell. If Kennamer was sane when he made that statement, then that is premeditated plan and he effected the death of John Gorrell.

"The defendant has interposed a plea of insanity. I think, gentlemen, it is folly to consume your time or the valuable time of this court in discussing the defense. But in fairness to the defendant, I want to call your attention to a few matters in that connection. I submit to you, gentlemen of this jury, at this moment in full confidence and with abiding faith in your judgment, have you ever listened to a more shrewd witness or one displaying more intelligence than Phil Kennamer?" says Rowe. "I have been in the practice of law, and it seems to have the thing to do to relate some of one's history, and during the time I have been in practicing law,

I can't recall a defendant exhibiting the calmness the defendant Phil Kennamer did on the stand, and my practice has been extensive. I say that if Phil Kennamer is insane, God pity these lawyers. I say that you are just as capable of judging a man sane or insane on that stand, even though you can't pronounce the 'hifalutin' words."

Rowe states in a commanding tone, "I say to you that it does not take an expert, and I feel like resenting for you that you are not intelligent enough to ascertain the facts in this case. You know how those streams of blood flow, and this expert said that a minute lapsed between those shots. Was that necessary to self-defense? Why was the second shot fired when the first would have killed him? Doesn't that indicate the fact that it was carrying out his threat to kill John Gorrell and to be sure that it was done?

"It will be argued, gentlemen, no doubt, that he was not armed, but he told you on the stand that he knew the custom of the deceased in carrying a pistol. I cannot help but join in that theory advanced that when he got out to that hospital and found the gun, he knew that it could be identified as John Gorrell's gun, and in an effort to commit that perfect crime, took it out and killed him. Shot him in self-defense. Why did he carefully take that gun and put it beside Gorrell's poor lifeless body? If he shot him in self-defense, intelligent and smart as he is, having been around courts practically all of his life, the natural thing to have done, and I believe Phil would have done it, would have been go to an officer, or call an officer, and say, 'I had to kill to save my life.' He would not have anything to fear, but he didn't do that. . . . The fact remains, notwithstanding all of that, that this defendant admitted practically everything to which Huff testified, didn't he?

"Gentlemen, these instructions will be with you, but I want to call your attention to this fact and this statement and that is, even if the kidnapping business were all true, the extortion business were all true, that would not justify Phil Kennamer in taking away the life of John Gorrell." With a matter-of-fact attitude, he says, "That is the law. The only thing in this case that would excuse you or warrant you in sending him back is that he must have been insane at the time, or that he killed in self-defense. That is the issue when you go to your jury box and take those instructions with you. Remember, they are the guide posts that direct you along your journey."

Rowe sinks heavily into his seat, after speaking for an hour and twelve minutes.

The jurymen sit stoned-faced and unmoved for most of the day while counsel gave their arguments, making it hard for spectators and attorneys alike to anticipate what they will decide about Phil's future.

The court is recessed at 5:33 PM.

Meanwhile, there are rumors that Jack Snedden and Randall Morton are under technical arrest in a hotel in connection with Sidney Born's death.

Jack laughs and says, "We understand that we're supposed to be arrested after the trial ends. We have our own theory about the Born death. We do not believe he committed suicide. We think he was murdered, and we have our idea who may have done it."

Jack declines to name names but is asked by a reporter whether it's a state witness. "No, we're the state witnesses supposed to be under suspicion."

One unnamed official says that he understands the boys are being guarded for safety, rather than as a preliminary to arrest. The sheriff's department has nothing to say about the Born case, other than that it has no suspects. Private investigators are still looking into Sidney's death.

Thursday, February 21

- Day 10 of the Trial — The Jury's Verdict -

Charles B. Stuart, the seventy-eight-year-old attorney from Oklahoma City, closes for the defense, despite feeling ill, and asks the court for its patience because of his condition.

"One of these gentlemen, Mr. King, made the statement . . . that I was here to represent the defendant and said I would weep and that every tear would be paid for. I am here without price. No sordid money is in my pocket in this case. I have known the father and son for many years. I have eaten his salt, and I have broken his bread. And when he called me to his side in his day of darkness, I was glad to be with him. I want you, therefore, to go with me patiently in this case because I know this will be the last word which will be said in this court for this boy, and I shall speak that word."

Stuart references Huff's story that Phil was planning to rent a plane, then kill Gorrell. "Phil Kennamer never ran a plane in his life, and yet Huff, good old Huff, says that Phil was going to take him up in a plane, have a parachute, knock Gorrell in the head, and jump out. Gorrell, then being unconscious, could not guide his plane and crash. That came out of old Huff's imagination. Dear old Huff."

Stuart begins to walk over to the prosecution's table and, in an impassioned tone, states, "I say to you in all your experience, if you think you can raise to any eminence in this case," he pounds the table in front of Gilmer, "by riding me, ride high, cowboy, ride high. The more we face the facts in this case, the more convinced we are this prosecution is a lot of guesswork. A lot of suspicion. You cannot convict any man because you guess he did it . . . convict any man on suspicion. The state must prove to you by reputable and definite testimony beyond a reasonable doubt this boy is guilty.

"May I say something more? They have pursued this boy. He has been the object of ridicule by the newspapers, and he came here in order that he might get a fair and impartial trial. They have chased this boy to the sacred temple of justice, and you must see to it that no prejudiced testimony shall enter this case by the poison-spewing of his enemies. I love a brave man, and I hate a coward. I believe that you are brave men, and, like brave and true men, you will tell this jury that this boy is not guilty."

Stuart demands acquittal on the grounds of self-defense and because Phil is mentally unbalanced. He tells the jury that it isn't their responsibility to confine Phil if he is insane and that it's the responsibility of Phil's father to see to it that Phil gets the treatment that he needs.

Mr. Stuart praises Phil for killing John Gorrell, whom he sees as an extortionist, and says that Phil's love for Virginia Wilcox was and still is overpowering, and that is the mainspring of this amazing case.

"This case to me is simple. It is not complicated in any sense. It is a plain tale told by the witnesses. Here's a young man grown up in a highly nervous state, reaching mental adolescence before the ordinary boy can read or write. It is the story of a boy's uncontrollable love for a girl and the story of that boy trying to prevent harm to that girl. I take very little interest in the youthful escapades of this boy. They make very little impression on me, except that four years ago he met a girl and she became at once the object of his affection. She had her first date with him."

Stuart addresses the jury: "Gentlemen, you can't discard the tremendous force and impulse love brings upon the human race. It is the strongest, most irresistible impulse among humans. For that feeling, men have been led to things that appear impossible.

"I take the position that the moving force that drove the boy to hold that dead boy accountable was the love for that girl. It's a living fact in the case. Among the many unkind remarks the distinguished ex-attorney general made was that the boy had two objects: one, to get the girl first, if he could, by attention and persuasion and love and to become the son-in-law of Wilcox money; second, that he'd kidnap her and get Wilcox money anyway. That boy had no idea of that. He dreamed of only one thing—to gain the love of Virginia. I don't know whether the Wilcoxes have any money; I don't care, but the assertion has been made that he was so low, so mean as to want to get the money.

"Gorrell said he was in favor of a kidnapping, but Kennamer said an extortion note was better. What Gorrell wanted was the easy money. He didn't care one iota what happened to the girl. He wrote the letter. It is one of the most cold-blooded, exact, brief, severe letters of extortion I have ever read," says Stuart, looking at the jurors.

"Kennamer told Jack Snedden that he knew Virginia was lost to him, 'but call her and ask her to write me a note,' he told Snedden. Virginia promised to write but didn't."

Stuart then picks up the letter that Phil wrote to Virginia and holds it up to the jurors. "This letter is one of self-abasement, of humiliation. He loved that girl, so he begged for the crumbs from the table. That letter tells of his troubles. He tells the girl, 'All I have for you is regard and admiration—the old feeling is dead—if we meet again I assure you it will be casually.' Those were the parting words of a boy in deep agony. Don't forget you can't be a boy again, and a boy can't be a man.

"But we have to face the facts in this case, and the more we face them, we realize the prosecution is sinking. You can't convict a man on suspicion. It must be proved by testimony beyond reasonable doubt that this boy is guilty.

"I want you to listen to me," Stuart says in a domineering voice. "If a man ever writes a letter to any of those I love demanding money and threatening death, I'd take my shotgun and cut him in two like a rattlesnake. And you'd do it, too, if the blood of your ancestors hasn't turned to water.

"When Phil got there at 19th and Utica, they say he slipped into Gorrell's car before Gorrell got there. That's not even good nonsense. That girl was checked in at 10:50. Phil Kennamer didn't leave where he was until 11. So that when Gorrell went out to his car, he was bound to have to take care of himself for fifteen or twenty minutes before Kennamer got there. They make Gorrell out to be a giant when Phil gets in the car with him and make him a mollycoddle and pigmy when Phil sees him in Kansas City. Will you believe me when I tell you the doctrine of self-defense does not depend on the statute? It is God-given, the right to protect one's own life.

"Is there a living person who has disputed the story of Phil Kennamer as to what happened in that car? He's the only living person who can tell you!" Stuart shouts. "They drove a little ways, and Gorrell asked him about the letter. Phil told him he wasn't going to mail the letter, that he's given it to the authorities. Gorrell drew this pistol and threw it in Kennamer's face. Kennamer believes the pistol snapped once. There was but three cartridges in the gun. When he pulled the trigger, it snapped. Kennamer grabbed his hands. They fought, each trying to turn on the other. Both had their fingers on the trigger. Phil finally shot and killed Gorrell.

"If that boy was irresponsible, you must, if you have any doubt, resolve that doubt in his favor. As to the right of self-defense, there can be no doubt. He was trying to keep that dead man from kidnapping that girl, and he thought that was the only way. Phil had a lot of companions. Every one of them knew that Phil was going to Kansas City. Not one of them believed he was going to kill Gorrell." Stuart turns and looks at Jack Snedden and others in the courtroom, then shouts, "If you knew it, why didn't you stop it?!"

Jack lowers his head, abashed. No one else believed Phil when he made the threats to kill John Gorrell. Besides, Jack and

Beebe did take the knife away from Phil and thought that he and Morton had stopped the potential killing.

"There's but one just verdict here. The state has previously said it wants the death penalty. The attorney general told you he personally doesn't ask it. He tells you to put him in the penitentiary for treatment. It's unjust. It's cruel. If this boy is entitled to his deliverance, let the future take care of itself. The responsibility isn't yours.

"I've spoken the last word in defense of the boy. I forgive the attorney general for everything but one thing. He said I would be paid for every tear I shed," Stuart says sarcastically. "No, general, you'd better listen to the jingle of money in your own pocket that you have taken for prosecuting this case."

Turning to the jurors, Stuart makes his final plea: "Be just and fear not. I hope when you return to your homes you find that peace and comfort I expect to find. Give this boy his deliverance."

After one hour and forty-five minutes, Stuart finishes his vehement rebuttal at 10:45 AM.

At 11 AM, W. F. "Dixie" Gilmer takes the last speaking position, after county attorney Holly Anderson decides at the last minute to give it to his thirty-three-year-old assistant. Gilmer states that the defense insists that Kennamer doesn't know right from wrong in one breath and then, in another, that he went to meet with Gorrell to persuade him not to kidnap Virginia Wilcox.

"This demolishes the insanity theory," says Gilmer, standing at the jury box with his hand on the rail.

"I'm handicapped in this. I won't attempt to match the wisdom of Judge Stuart," he says earnestly. "That would be ridiculous for me to try. I can't answer his argument because I saw nothing of an argument in it. I want you to believe me when I say the state has tried to be fair in this case. I want to be fair to Phil Kennamer and his father." Then he shouts, "But I want to be fair to the parents of that poor dead boy, too!"

The jurors and the spectators perk up, as Gilmer makes his emotional case to seek justice for the Gorrells.

"When Phil Kennamer, at the age of five, was talking about 'hangman's noose,' John Gorrell was in kindergarten. When Phil Kennamer was running away from school, John Gorrell was going right ahead. The only thing Phil Kennamer finished in his life was murder. Stuart said, 'Let's tear off the veil.' I'm going to." Gilmer paces back and forth in front of the jury box and pounds on the railing, while raising his voice to make his points. Periodically, he nervously wipes his hands on his handkerchief.

"If everything they say is true, you will say whether the arrogant, supercilious son of the federal judge has the right to put himself in the seat of the judge, the jury, and the Almighty and say to John Gorrell—'You must die.' He hasn't the right to do that, and you know it.

"I want to spend three minutes on this insanity plea. Judge Stuart says, 'Toss out the experts.' All right, out they go," as he makes a sweeping motion with his hand. "Then Mr. Moss asks you to trace the narrow line of sanity—does he know right from wrong? He tells you, bless your hearts, that Phil went out there to prevent a wrong, the kidnapping of Virginia Wilcox. And they tell you Kennamer didn't know right from wrong! The defendant said he knew right from wrong.

"Stuart asks why we didn't use Pres Cochran? The record shows Pres was the first witness the defense subpoenaed. About Doctor Knoblock. He explained simply to you about those two shots being fired at a minute interval. When that second shot was fired into the quivering body of John Gorrell, already dead, it removed any self-defense from this case. We have to consider all the actions of the defendant. There is nothing vicious going to enter this lawsuit against John Gorrell. I wish I had the ability of Moss and could inject names like Bruno Hauptmann. But you have the picture of a pampered wastrel killer, kidnapper. Kennamer. There he sits." He casts his open hand at Phil.

Phil looks stoic, as Gilmer draws attention to him. Many look at Phil to gauge his reaction, only to be disappointed.

"We all agreed that he has to be put somewhere. He can't walk out of the door a free man. I'll tell you in a few moments where to put him. This is of vital importance.

"Mr. McCollum wanted us to answer several questions. One of them was, what about a motive? When a man says ten days ahead, 'I'm going to kill this man,' and kills him, and after seeing his lawyer say, 'I did kill him,' he has to have a motive. I'm not interested in a motive, though. The killing of Gorrell occurred just as Kennamer said it would. That's enough. The body of John Gorrell was found Thanksgiving night. The papers were full of it the next day. Two days later, the papers said the son of a jurist was suspected. Then he realized he was caught and decided to surrender. He couldn't run away. He needed his father's help. I don't believe Flint Moss and Judge Stuart can fool this jury. The only way they can win this lawsuit is to fool you.

"Who started talking of the kidnapping and killings? Kennamer. That's the first word of testimony you heard, that Kennamer was going to kill. He told Cadillac Booth of easy money and kidnappings, he shows all the way through he has criminal tendencies and was abnormal. He started the whole thing. We all know he did. At every stage Kennamer was in it.

"You can turn the man loose, but what's the effect on society?" he asks rhetorically. "You're going to have two classes of young people, one inherently good, the other bad. What will the good class think? They'll think that if the son of a federal judge can be turned loose, what's the use? If you turn the boy loose, you turn upside-down the ideals of the youth in this country. I think this murder is an indictment on the parents of those children over there in Tulsa. I think a lot of them haven't done their best in rearing those children."

Gilmer wants to win this case, and if it means indirectly condemning Phil's parents for this murder, then so be it. He is willing to pull out all of the stops to get a conviction. Besides, bad parenting has been blamed for these wealthy and seemingly out-of-control children getting into trouble, and this opinion has already been made public by Mayor Penney of Tulsa. A guilty plea by the jury could be just the thing to give these parents pause about how they're raising their children and to make the parents rein them in.

"I'm going to close. What should you do with this defendant? You're older than I am. My suggestion is just a suggestion. They all say he should be confined. There are just two state insane hospitals in Oklahoma, and the heads of those told you there is no place there for Kennamer. As sure as you send him to the penitentiary, the natural reaction on the part of his father will be to try and get him out. On behalf of the state of Oklahoma, we're asking you to send the boy to the electric chair in the same calm deliberation he used in sending John Gorrell into eternity."

At 11:55 AM, Judge Hurst recesses the court for lunch The members of the jury eat lunch in their mostly unfurnished conference room, due to lack of funds after completion of the courthouse, then begin their deliberation in one of four rooms on the fourth floor at 12:40 PM. Bailiff Trees, who has the only key, locks the jurors in the room, while Bailiff Frank Goodwin stands guard. Another bailiff is posted on the third-floor landing that leads to the jury room.

Outside the courtroom, Judge Kennamer paces the hallway for a time, then sits and chats with friends. He leaves to go to his room at the Graham Hotel. Doctor Gorrell hangs around for a while in the hall and takes this opportunity to ask reporters for a little privacy while his family deals with the loss of their son. Just after the case goes to the jury, Dr. Gorrell suffers a nervous breakdown in his room at the Pawnee Hotel, a result of the strain he has been under since the murder of his son. Mrs. Gorrell is also in tears, attempting to console her husband.

Here are five young Tulsa men, asking each other what the verdict would be in the Kennamer case. Left to right are Ed Gessler, John Newlin, Jack Snedden, George Reynolds and Randall Morton. Snedden testified as to a letter Kennamer wrote to Miss Virginia Wilcox, with whom Kennamer said he had been infatuated, and later said that Kennamer had threatened him as he left the stand. Morton told of taking a knife from Kennamer shortly before the killing. The picture was taken at Pawnee before the verdict came in.

(l to r) Friends Ed Gessler, John Newlin, Jack Snedden, George
Reynolds, and Randall Morton, chatting just before the verdict comes in.
(courtesy of Jason Morrow)

"Mrs. Gorrell and I should now like to be relieved of the pitiless publicity that has of necessity pursued us since the tragedy that deprived us of our boy. We have done what we could do to cooperate with the proper authorities in the presentation of the case, to the courts. We find no fault with the trial through its several stages and shall accept the verdict of the court and jury, as parents should, who have no other refuge in periods of grief as great as ours has been. Our only emotion toward Judge and Mrs. Kennamer is one of deepest sympathy. Whatever the result, we trust no Tulsa father or mother shall ever be called upon to sustain the sacrifice we have made. Perhaps the result may bring an awakening. John would want us to be brave under such circumstances. We shall strive to be so in memory of him. For our sake, please let the press and public conclude that with the final expression of the courts, the tragedy shall remain sealed only within our own hearts." Dr. Gorrell then leaves the courthouse for his room in the Pawnee Hotel.

The waiting game begins. Some reporters amuse themselves by taking possession of the judge's desk and starting a game of bridge. One reporter takes a nap beside the counsel table and is rudely awakened later when some of his associates flash a camera bulb in his face. A reporter's wife plays with the judge's gavel. Between 5:30 and 7 PM, the jurors recess for dinner and stretch their legs with a walk for a few blocks, then return to the fourth floor of the courthouse to resume their deliberations.

At 9:05 PM, not long after dinner, the jurors are ready to come back to court. The guards won't say whether it's because the jury needs additional information or a verdict has been reached. Judge Hurst is called from his home, which is eleven blocks from the courthouse. Soon, Judge Kennamer, his son Franklin, his daughter Opal, and his son-in-law, Russell Hayes, come into the courtroom and seat themselves at the council table. State attorney Holly Anderson and his assistant, W. F. Gilmer, enter the courtroom and remain standing, while Dr. Gorrell takes a seat at the prosecutors' table.

Sheriff C. M. Burkdoll brings in the pale-faced prisoner, Phil Kennamer, at 9:13 PM. Newspaper reporters begin taking flash pictures of Phil and are immediately ejected from the courtroom by deputies. Phil scowls at the reporters, then turns to smile at his father, who maintains a serious look. The jurors are brought in. They hold their hats in their hands, signifying they have reached a verdict. Otherwise, their hats would still be in the chambers if they needed additional information.

Judge Hurst takes his seat just seconds after the jurors are seated. He reminds the court of an earlier rule that no photos will be permitted. Facing the jurors, he asks, "Gentlemen of the jury, have you reached your verdict?"

"We have," answers Foreman Jacob Clark.

"You may return it."

Clark hands the verdict to Bailiff Trees, who then gives it to the court reporter, C. J. Harry. The verdict is given to Judge Hurst, who reads it to himself, then hands it to the Pawnee County District Court clerk, Mrs. Nora Harshbarger. She rises and in a slow, deliberate voice reads the verdict:

> In the district court, Pawnee County, state of Oklahoma. State of Oklahoma versus Phil Kennamer, case number 1784 verdict. We the jury, drawn and sworn to try the issues in the above mentioned cause, do upon our oaths find the defendant guilty of manslaughter in the first degree as charged in the instruction, and being unable to agree upon the punishment leave the penalty to be assessed by the court. Signed Jacob Clark, foreman.

Phil's face is stoic as he stares at the jury box. Judge Kennamer lowers his eyes and drops his hands in his lap. He appears crushed by the verdict.

"Let the verdict be filed," orders Judge Hurst.

The judge calls Mr. Anderson and Mr. McCollum to the bench, where a quiet consultation takes place.

"Sentence will be passed at two o'clock Saturday afternoon," says the judge. He thanks the jurors for their service, and court is recessed.

The people in the courtroom begin to talk, and some applaud. Opal walks over to Phil, smiles sadly, and shakes his hand. Neither Phil nor his father makes any comment. The sheriff leads Phil from the courtroom by his right arm, back to the county jail.

"It's just one of those things," comments Phil.

Mr. McCollum, the only member of the defense team who is in court when the verdict is read, does not make any public comment. In the hallway, scores of people congratulate Gilmer and Anderson for a job well done, and the only public statement made is "The state of Oklahoma is entirely satisfied."

After the verdict was read, Doctor Gorrell, John's father, says, "I'm very happy over the outcome of this lawsuit. I appreciate what you gentlemen [the prosecution] have done. I know that Judge Hurst will see that justice is done.

"We find no fault with the trial through its several stages and shall accept the verdict of the court and jury as parents should, who have no other refuge in periods of grief as great as ours has been. Our only emotion toward Judge and Mrs. Kennamer is one of deepest sympathy."

Defense attorney Moss says that the jury's verdict is "Terrible. . . . It was substantially against the fair import of the evidence."

Judge Kennamer will not tell the reporters how Phil is taking the news but does remark, "You might say the case is still pending at this stage. There are things coming up yet, which might have a bearing, and I don't think you should talk to Phil until after the sentence. You can see him then, as I want to be as nice to you as possible."

It is rumored that the jury was not convinced at any time that Phil was insane, as the defense attorneys tried to prove. They did agree, without difficulty, that Phil was guilty of murder but could not agree on the length of his prison term and decided to leave it to the court. The death penalty was off the table, because it required all twelve ballots to get that verdict. The first ballot was 9 to 3 in favor of conviction. Those three were for acquittal, one vote for the insanity plea, and the other two for self-defense.

"One of the jurors wanted to make it ninety-nine years," says jury foreman Jacob Clark.

Now the court is mandated to grant Phil bail, but how much for his temporary release is still in question. His defense attorneys will file a motion for a new trial. If it's denied, the notice of appeal will be given, and an appeal bond will be set.

Friday, February 22

Today is Washington's birthday, a holiday, and most government offices are closed. It appears as if the city of Pawnee is returning to normal. The restaurants are not jammed with hungry people, the courthouse is almost deserted, and there is plenty of parking around it.

As reported by his jailers, Phil sits in his jail cell, seemingly unconcerned about the punishment that awaits him from Judge Hurst. Moss tells Phil he will file an appeal, so he expects Phil to be released on bail soon. Newspapermen are not allowed in the jail to interview Phil, as per Judge Kennamer's request. It is said from jail sources that when Phil was returned to his cell Friday night, he told the other prisoners: "Well, I got manslaughter. That's what I thought it would be."

One of the prisoners thinks Phil is joking because he acts so apathetic. Phil later convinces him that the verdict is true.

As for Phil's attorneys, they will likely file a motion for a new trial, which they fully expect to be denied. Then they will appeal the verdict in the Criminal Court of Appeals. The Court of Appeals will evaluate the trial to see whether the jury heard any evidence that was not legally admissible and whether the judge omitted any evidence that was pertinent to the case.

After the verdict was read, Anderson says, "You may quote me as believing that there is no reversible error in the record of the Kennamer trial. I believe that Judge Hurst held closely to the law, resolving every doubt in favor of the defendant as the law requires."

Judge Hurst will set the bail, and that amount will be the number of years that Phil will serve, multiplied by $1,000. Yet speculation surrounds what Judge Hurst will decide regarding how much time Phil will serve in prison. It could be as few as four years up to life in prison.

County attorney Holly Anderson says that his office will not reopen the investigation into the death of Sidney Born. "I'm thoroughly convinced it was suicide. If there are going to be any arrests by private investigators, I have not been informed."

At the end of the Kennamer trial, Dr. Born believes that an arrest is imminent of at least one of the two suspected slayers.

On an interesting note, a huge dust storm is engulfing many states, including Oklahoma. Many of the reporters heading back to Tulsa encounter "a heavy fog of dust the entire 60 miles with headlights piercing it for a short distance ahead," with winds sustained at 25 to 28 mph. Kansas, Nebraska, Colorado, Oklahoma, Wyoming, and many other states are affected. The dust is so thick that the sky grows dark by mid afternoon, and the streetlights turn on.

Saturday, February 23

- Day 11 of the Trial — The Punishment -

The court opens at 2 PM, and a capacity crowd is in attendance to hear the sentence Judge Hurst will impose on Phil. Most of today's crowd consists of the Pawnee locals, but the usual attendees from Tulsa who occupied the front row of the courtroom, including Virginia Wilcox, are not present.

The defense attorneys have tried for nearly two hours to delay the sentencing. Defense attorney Moss has filed a motion for a new trial, citing fifteen reasons. The main reason is a remark that Dixie Gilmer, the assistant Tulsa County prosecutor, made, that only the wealthy citizens of Tulsa could get front-row seats in the courtroom during the trial. And Gilmer also whispered to the jury at times. In addition, Moss contends that the state attempted to paint John Gorrell as a good citizen, after it was agreed on in Judge Hurst's chambers that it was not permissible, and this deserves a new trial. Moss continues with his other reasons and even takes swipes at the judge's handling of a witness and suggesting to the jury that Kennamer should be confined to a mental institution. Judge Hurst denies he was influencing the jury and says he was asking the witness to clarify his answer.

Judge Hurst says, "I think this man has had as fair a trial as he could have. The motion for a new trial is overruled."

The judge turns to attorney Holly Anderson for his recommendation for punishment.

"Evidence shows no insanity, that this murder was premeditated for at least seven or eight days. The jury, however, brought in a verdict of manslaughter; the state asks that the court give this defendant ninety-nine years."

Defense attorney James A. McCollum weighs in on Kennamer's punishment: "Your honor has a disagreeable task. We all wish the jury had fixed sentence. I'm going to tell you what I think the evidence and proof shown calls for. I don't think there is any question but what this defendant is seriously mentally sick. He is nineteen years of age. Soon he passes from boyhood to manhood. He is the victim of an unfortunate circumstance, not a confirmed criminal. I believe I am expressing the views of this boy's father. He should be confined, but not until all hope of his life and manhood is gone. We should not be swept off our feet and 'plant him' just 'count him out' from here on.

"I don't think he should be sent to Granite. There's a bunch of unruly lads there," continues McCollum. "We agree that since this unfortunate thing must be done, it must be the penitentiary, where he can be under medical observation and treatment." He finishes by saying that Kennamer should serve a minimum sentence of four years.

Judge Hurst has heard from both sides regarding what Kennamer's sentence should be and has now made a decision. At 3:45, Judge Hurst calls Phil to his feet: "The defendant stand up!"

Phil rises and takes a bold step to stand in front of the bench, with his hands clasped behind his back, while the judge gives him a stern lecture before passing his sentence.

"Through the trial of this case, the court has tried to be absolutely fair. You made an application before the court for a change of venue from your county where you live and where the crime was committed, and where the deceased lived, and the court granted the change."

Phil nods at Judge Hurst in agreement. He stands very still and erect, with his heels together, while the sentence is being pronounced. His face is bloodless, as he stares directly into Judge Hurst's eyes, prepared to receive his punishment.

"Now throughout the trial here in Pawnee, the court has tried to give you every right and protect your every right. A good jury, as good a jury as I have ever seen in a courtroom, has tried your case. I personally have known quite a number of them for many years, and I know them to be men of honor and men of sound judgment.

"They have heard the evidence on both sides and the argument of council, and they have rejected your plea of insanity and self-defense, and they have given you the benefit of the doubt on the question of premeditation, and by their verdict they have held that you did not kill with a premeditative design. I think the reason the jury did that was because you went to the scene where you met the deceased unarmed and you killed the deceased with his own gun. That is the only theory on which the jury could have found no premeditation. The evidence would have justified the jury in finding premeditation," says Judge Hurst.

"It was suggested that the state wants to punish you to injure your father. It was also suggested that you might not be given the same trial as anyone else. In my idea, the son of a federal judge and the son of a peasant should be treated alike. It is our theory that every man stands equal before the law.

"Unfortunately, it's the innocent who suffer more than the guilty," lectures the judge. "Your act brought heartache to two families, both of them innocent. I've observed that while your father was broken-hearted, you yourself have shown little concern during this trial. I've been shocked at that. Maybe you haven't betrayed your real feelings.

"I prefer the jury had set the punishment in this case by using its composite judgment. I ought not to give you one minute more or less by reason of your father. It would be dangerous to society to turn you out too soon. If I give you too much and the experts' theory of your mental illness is correct, the sentence can be remedied. It is therefore the judgment of the court that you serve twenty-five years in McAlester prison."

Moss whispers, "Sit down, Phil."

Phil turns and seats himself at the counsel's table. The lawyer tells the court that he will immediately appeal and asks that Phil be granted bail. Judge Hurst allows a $25,000 bail to be filed in five days. Moss asks for ten days, and the judge grants the request.

"That will be all," says the judge, and with a rap of his gavel, the trial of Phil Kennamer is over. The crowd, in a flurry of loud conversation, clears out of the courtroom. Phil is taken to the sheriff's office before returning to jail to answer questions from newspaper reporters.

Judge Kennamer is not in court when the sentence is handed down, but he tells a United Press reporter that he favors an appeal in the case.

Dr. John Gorrell, the victim's father, says, "I am satisfied with the sentence. I am satisfied with the verdict and the sentence. The judgment of the court is my judgment, as I said before the verdict came in."

Fifteen minutes after he hears his sentence, Phil shakes hands with a *Tulsa Tribune* reporter, lights a cigarette, and sits on a bench.

"So far as the closing statement of Judge Hurst is concerned, it was fair," Phil says. "He made every effort to conduct the trial in a fair, rigidly impartial manner. . . . I deeply regret the occurrence of this tragedy, not in its ultimate effect on me, but its effect on the innocent parties involved—my family and that of Gorrell.

"Based on the record in the case, the evidence introduced, I have little quarrel with Judge Hurst's sentence. I feel, though, that it was not a trial in the ordinary sense of the word, but more approached the semblance of a Roman holiday. The clamor set up in the press at the outset was of such a nature it was impossible to find twelve men whose minds were free of bias. I think the jury was representative of an intelligent and honest citizenship, but in their subconscious minds had been poured such a stream of virus, it was impossible for them to be impartial.

"For Messieurs King, Anderson, Gilmer, and Wallace, I have only the deepest contempt. Those gentlemen for the state engaged in every low practice known to the courts, from intimidation of witnesses to introduction of extraneous matters, which were intended only to prejudice the minds of the jury. In its final analysis, the issues were not drawn between the state and this defendant but between the corrupt element and this defendant's family. The aim was not to destroy me but to destroy my father's honor."

Monday, February 25

Phil tells his jailers that he is ready to begin his prison term in McAlester. What he doesn't know is that his attorneys and his father, Franklin Kennamer, decided it was best not to make bond for Phil's protection.

Attorney C. B. Stuart makes a statement tonight: "We think that the boy is better off in prison while the case is being appealed. If he were released, this conviction would be hanging over him while he was out. As it is, we believe that the conviction will be reversed and that Phil will walk away from McAlester penitentiary in a few months a free man.

"It is better that he spend those few months in prison, then walk out with his name cleared," Stuart says. "We are supremely confident of a reversal in the case. We think it wise not to release him now. That was my advice to his father, and he has agreed to follow it.

"There were many errors which we believe will set aside the conviction. Making the bond would be no difficulty at all. There have been hundreds of friends of the family who offered to post bond."

Even thought he has until March 5 to make bond, Phil could be moved to McAlester in a few days, but the law states that Phil cannot be moved to prison until ten days have passed or unless Phil and his council waive his rights.

- Phil is Imprisoned -

Monday, March 4, 1935

Phil leaves the jail at 7:10 AM for the state pen in McAlester. Major Gordon W. Lillie "Pawnee Bill," an old friend of Phil's father, uses his big car for the 150-mile trip with Phil, Sheriff Burkdoll, and Deputy Joe Myers (*Brownsville Herald*, March 4, 1935).

Sheriff Burkdoll, Phil Kennamer, and "Pawnee Bill" at the McAlester
Prison.
(courtesy of Jason Morrow)

Phil Kennamer's prison booking photo.

Saturday, March 9

Detective Henry Maddux has made a statement that the bullets that killed John Gorrell are from different guns. It could be said that because Homer and Jack are close friends of Phil's, a delusional and conspiracy-driven Maddux believes that either of these two young men may have been involved in the death of Gorrell. There has been no evidence that points to the two shots to Gorrell's head coming from two different weapons. Yet Maddux is determined to proceed with this witch-hunt, despite expert testimony during the trial.

Prosecutor Dixie Gilmer has reopened the case and asks for Homer Wilcox's .22 caliber gun and Jack Snedden's .38 caliber for examination. Jack's brother, George, brings the weapon to Gilmer, saying it's the only gun Jack owns. Both weapons will be sent to the Department of Justice for a ballistics comparison and, Gilmer hopes, to emphatically put to rest the idea that the bullets that killed John Gorrell came from two different weapons, ruling out Jack's and Homer's.

Gilmer is also asking for clarification of a report from J. Edgar Hoover, director of the FBI, on the examination of the fatal bullets. It reads, ". . . no identification bullets with test bullet are each other. Fatal shell identical with test shell." Gilmer calls the telegram "confusing," and the FBI never clarifies it, even after Gilmer's request (*Brownsville Herald*, March 10, 1935, pg. 29).

Monday, March 11

Edna Harman is found guilty of contempt. Judge Hurst sentences her to thirty days in the county jail and a fine of $250. The punishment may have ended her days as a professional witness, because no further public information is available about her life and career. She dies on May 23, 1958, in San Diego, California.

Tuesday, April 2

Prentiss Rowe is elected mayor of Pawnee, Oklahoma.

Friday, April 19

This evening, Sergeant Henry Maddux resigns from the Tulsa police force. He says he was forced out by the police commissioner, Colonel Hoop, due to a police department scandal involving the Kennamer investigation. He was told by Hoop that the grand jury was going to indict him for concealing information about the case, including any obscene photos taken of young society girls. Both Hoop and Maddux have been questioned by a grand jury about Maddux's $25,000 bribe to "soft petal" certain angles of the investigation and for the way the investigation into Sidney Born's death was handled. Maddux says he will fight to keep his job and will appeal to the commission for a trial (*San Antonio Express*, April 20, 1935, pg. 3).

Monday, April 22

Phil is brought from prison in McAlester to Tulsa to testify before a grand jury about the deaths of John Gorrell and Sidney Born. After three hours of testimony and spurred by the mystery of the prominent youths' deaths, subpoenas are issued for Wade Thomas and Ted Bath (*San Antonio Express*, April 23, 1935, pg. 2). What Phil tells the jury is not disclosed, and prosecutors refuse to say which new evidence Phil reveals. There is no indictment for either Thomas or Bath, and no trial transpires.

Wednesday, April 24

The grand jury decides that the bribery and compromising photos can be branded as "exaggerations." The jury states, "We have been unable to ascertain the existence at any time of any nude, compromising, or obscene pictures involving any people connected with the case, and we are of the opinion that no such pictures existed. We found no evidence of a $25,000 bribe having been offered to anyone." About the death of Born, the grand jury charges that Henry Maddux failed to make a "complete and proper investigation into the death of Sidney Born Jr." The report also states, "At the present time, the grand jury is unable to determine whether Sidney Born Jr. committed suicide or was murdered" (*San Antonio Express*, April 25, 1935, pg. 3).

Tuesday, May 21

Phil is released from prison on a $25,000 appeal bond (*Pittsburgh Post Gazette*, May 22, 1935, pg. 1). Six friends of the Kennamer family put the money together for the bond, including Phil's brother-in-law, Russell Hayes. Phil says he plans to rest at the family farm in Chelsea and do some fishing.

Saturday, June 15

Phil's attorney files an appeal in Oklahoma City, alleging that there were nineteen errors in the trial. They want a reversal of the conviction and a new trial (*Brownsville Herald*, June 16, 1935, pg. 1).

Chapter 4
1936

- Appeal and Parole -

Friday, March 20

Phil is given a fifteen-day extension, so that his attorneys have more time to file a rehearing before the Criminal Court of Appeals. Phil is free until April 6 (*San Antonio Express*, March 21, 1936).

Monday, April 13

The assistant prosecutor of Tulsa County receives a telegram from Jack Snedden, who is attending the Hun School in Princeton, New Jersey.

"I have just learned that part of the evidence upon which Kennamer seeks a new trial is based on the premise that my testimony was untrue and that I was intoxicated when Kennamer was disarmed and that I was afraid to tell the truth. Those allegations are of course maliciously false. Last summer, Phil approached me and requested that I change my testimony. Because of my refusal, my family and I have been subject to indignities. All my statements on and off the witness stand were absolutely true." The defense team says that Jack told the jailer, Marion Hamby, that he was "afraid" to tell the truth (*San Antonio Express*, April 13, 1936).

Friday, April 17

Phil loses his appeal for a new trial. His defense team contends that Gilmer's closing remarks were "inflammatory and prejudicial" and that "sensational new evidence" has surfaced, which warrants a new trial. The criminal court of appeals disagrees, saying that Phil did get a fair trial, and states that he must serve a twenty-five-year sentence in prison. Phil is ordered to report back to prison by Wednesday, April 22 (*Ada Weekly News*, April 23, 1936 pg. 3).

Wednesday, April 22

Phil returns to prison. He dashes up the prison steps, past the reporters and the photographers. He tells Warden Roy Kenny, "Well, I've come back to stay awhile" (*San Antonio Express*, April 23, 1936).

Saturday, October 3

Virginia Wilcox and Jack Snedden marry at the Wilcox home. The small private ceremony is attended only by the Wilcox and Snedden families. With Phil in prison, it's not known whether he is aware of the wedding or what his reaction is.

Friday, October 30

Charles Stuart dies in Oklahoma City after a long illness. He was seventy-nine years old (*Ada Weekly News*, November 5, 1936).

Chapter 5
1937–1938

- In and Out of Prison -

1937

Saturday, July 24

Oklahoma governor Ernest W. Marland receives a resolution protesting clemency for Phil Kennamer from the Delaware County Anti-Thief Association. He passes it on to Fred Cunningham, the state pardon and parole attorney (*Ada Weekly News*, July 29, 1937).

Monday, October 18

Phil appears before the state sanity board for a routine examination (*Ada Weekly News*, October 21, 1937). Dr. Charles Pearce, chairman of the board, says there will be no statement until an official report is made. If the findings of that exam were reported, the results cannot be located, as of this writing.

1938

Saturday, January 22

Phil, twenty-two, says he wants to be a "man without a country" and live in South America, where he's been offered a job. "All I want to do is to get away from here and get this thing behind me and forget it. If I were released and it were possible under the terms of my release, I would leave the country permanently" (*San Antonio Express*, January 23, 1938).

Saturday, February 5

Phil has sent a letter to Horace Ballaine, Pawnee County attorney, demanding that a key prosecution witness be charged with perjury. Although no name is mentioned, Ballaine says that he will "check into it thoroughly," but unless "more definitive information were obtained, he doesn't feel disposed at this time to file such a charge" (*Albuquerque Journal*, February 6, 1938, pg. 1).

Wednesday, August 10

Phil has a new job in prison, working in the Treasury Department, which is said to be one of the best posts in prison (*Ada Weekly News*, August 11, 1938, pg. 7). His duties probably involve assisting the prison treasurer in the day-to-day operations of the prison.

Wednesday, August 17

Governor Marland is considering a parole for Phil. "I have made up my mind on the case, but I haven't made up my mind about what is best for society." Dr. Gorrell says, "I really do not feel the boy has been punished sufficiently for the crime he committed. I sincerely hope Governor Marland will not parole Phil Kennamer" (*El Paso Herald-Post*, August 17, 1938, pg. 1).

Thursday, October 27

Phil's mother is very ill, and Franklin Kennamer is requesting a parole for his son. Oklahoma governor Ernest W. Marland will consider an open hearing on October 31 (*Ada Weekly News*, October 27, 1938).

Monday, October 31

Franklin Kennamer's wish comes true: Governor Marland approves clemency for Phil (*Lawrence Journal World*, October 31, 1938, pg. 2).

Tuesday, November 1

Phil has a sanity board hearing at the McAlester Prison, in which he requests six months of parole to visit his sick mother in Arizona. The meeting takes two hours in the warden's office. The governor asks the parole sponsors, John Mabee, John Catlett, and Clarence Wright, to come to Oklahoma City for a meeting. "The parole will be prepared when they get here. I'm going to ask them to accept their responsibility in writing." Then the case is sent to Governor Marland for approval (*San Antonio Express*, November 2, 1938).

Wednesday, November 2

Governor Marland approves the Parole Board's findings and allows a six-month parole "on purely humanitarian grounds." Phil will travel to Phoenix, Arizona, to be with his mother and work on an oil company ranch. It's not known what responsibilities he will have. When asked whether he thinks Phil should be returned to prison after six months, the governor replies, "Maybe I can give you an unofficial opinion six months from now." This is an odd, noncommittal reply but perhaps typical for a politician, who doesn't want to deal with public criticism while he's still in office. His term ends on January 9, 1939 (*San Antonio Express*, November 2, 1938, pg. 3).

Wednesday, November 9

Phil leaves the McAlester prison today, and it causes quite a stir in Tulsa among politicians, religious leaders, and public officials, who voice their opinions on the issue: "Should prison gates swing open for the son of an austere federal judge to comfort a supposedly dying mother?" (*Nevada State Journal*, November 13, 1938, pg. 3).

Chapter 6
1939

- Parole Board Abolished -

January 1939

Holly L. Anderson begins his first term in the Oklahoma House of Representatives.

Monday, January 9

Leon C. Phillips begins his term as governor of Oklahoma.

Monday, January 16

The new pardon and parole attorney, J. A. Minton, announces that the unofficial pardon and parole board will be abolished. "The board's deliberations entail a great amount of work for this office. It depends largely on investigations made by the pardon and parole attorney, who really should make the decisions." Minton also says that the public hearings will cease, because they pit one community against the other, and the Phil Kennamer case is one example (*Ada Weekly News*, January 19, 1939).

Thursday, March 9

Governor Phillips will decide whether Phil should complete his twenty-five-year sentence (*Ada Weekly News*, March 9, 1939, pg. 1).

Sunday, March 12

Phil's mother, Lillie Kennamer, dies at age fifty-four in Tulsa (*Ada Weekly News*, March 16, 1939, pg. 3).

Tuesday, May 2

Phil's six-month parole is finished, but Governor Leon Phillips grants him a one-month parole extension. "Because of the press of State business, additional time is required in which to make a thorough and complete study of the case before taking final action," says the governor (*San Antonio Express*, May 3, 1939).

Monday, May 29

Governor Phillips denies Phil's parole application, saying he read the record and believes Phil received a fair trial (*Nevada State Journal*, May 30, 1939, pg. 3).

Friday, June 2

After being paroled for seven months, Phil returns to prison by order of Governor Phillips (*Prescott Evening Courier*, June 3, 1939, pg. 2).

Chapter 7
1943

-Phil's Waiver and Army Training -

Monday, January 11

Robert S. Kerr begins his term as governor of Oklahoma.

Wednesday, April 21

Phil, with his father by his side, is granted parole by the three-man state clemency board. County attorney Dixie Gilmer and Dr. John Gorrell bitterly argue against that decision. Dr. Gorrell is choked with emotion, while pleading to the board to require "this killer of my son" to "serve his term the same as any other convict." The board, however, does reject the plea for a pardon. Governor Robert Kerr says he will follow the board's recommendation for parole. Phil tells reporters after the decision, "The only thought I have in mind is that I want everything I say and do to vindicate fully the courage and kindness of the gentlemen of the board and the governor" (*Ada Weekly News*, April 22, 1943).

Tuesday, May 4

Oklahoma governor Robert S. Kerr grants Phil his parole and signs a waiver of civil custody, a required procedure, in order for Phil to join the armed forces. Phil will be sent to Fort Benning, Georgia, for parachute training (*Ada Weekly News*, May 6, 1943).

Chapter 8
1944

- Phil's Premonition -

Tuesday, February 22

Phil comes to Oklahoma City to testify at a clemency conspiracy trial of former governor Leon Phillips, who is accused of taking $500 of an $8,000 parole payoff. Phil is expected to testify about his conversations with Governor Phillips while serving time in the McAlester prison and his own parole. [*Note*: Former governor Phillips is acquitted by a 9 to 3 vote of the jury.] Phil has just finished training at a paratrooper school. He speaks with the managing editor of the *Tulsa World*, Edward D. Burke, and says, "Something just seems to tell me that I won't come back. I hope that if I die under the flag of my country, those who have condemned me will hold me differently in their memories."

Phil Kennamer (r) and Attorney George Miskovsky in 1943 before Phil
testifies before the Fitzgerald conspiracy trial
(Courtesy of the Gateway to Oklahoma History)

Phil Kennamer after the Fitzgerald conspiracy trial in 1943.
(courtesy of the Gateway to Oklahoma History.)
Photo Credit: Bill Stockwell

Monday, May 8

An excerpt from "As I See It" by Milton D. Rogers, S/Sgt. (ret.) of the 517th Parachute Regimental Combat Team in 2007:

We got on the train and went to Camp Patrick Henry, Virginia, close to the seaport of Newport News. We moved into the barracks and went thru the processing that never ends. My 23rd birthday happened there, and the bunch I hung with decided to have a party. They took up a collection and bought some beer and some pop, and the party was underway in the barracks.

Phil Kennamer decided we needed sandwiches. I said, "There's no place to get anything here." He said, "There's that mess hall right over there. . . . Follow my lead and do what I tell you." They went to the mess hall. The cooks had piles of baked hams they were slicing off the bone to serve for lunch or dinner the next day. The meat was on huge platters, piled high. He said to the accomplice, "Pick up an armful of those bread loaves and follow me." The kid did so.

A cook got between Kennamer and the door, and Kennamer said, "Get out of my way, you @#$%, or I'll break your @#$% knee." The cook got out of the way, and the raiding party returned triumphant. When he decided we really needed mustard, too, we restrained them from going back. It was a dandy fine birthday and going away party. . . .

It took about two weeks to reach Naples, Italy. The sea was relatively smooth and the weather was warm. We got a pitch game (a trick-taking card game) going on the deck, Washburn and Burnham against Phil Kennamer and me (Milton Rogers). There are several thousand varieties of pitch, but the same game is played in Oklahoma and Tennessee as is played in Blanding and Bluff, Utah. I was on the losing side most of the time because my partner overbid his hand severely. He wouldn't let anybody else win the bid. We made fun of him and reviled him. He named us those SOBs from Utah. In Army language, that is almost a compliment.

Kennamer was on night KP (kitchen patrol) for part of the trip. He went down the first night reviling the Utahans. There was a merchant marine in charge of the kitchen, his second in command being Sergeant Prill, our own battalion mess sergeant. His cooking fit the army term "mess" real well. Anyway, this merchant seaman said, "What part of Utah are those guys from?" Kennamer said, "A hick town you never heard of named Blanding." The merchantman said, "Heard of? I was in the cc camp cooking for two years. Go get those guys." Kennamer came and got us, and down in the galley we went. Sergeant Prill saw us coming and said, "If you guys are going to stay here, you're going to work." The merchantman said, "They are my guests and they are not going to work." Instead of gaining three more hands, Prill lost Kennamer. It wasn't much of a loss, because he wasn't much for work anyway.

Tuesday, June 6, 1944   D-Day

Tuesday, August 15

During Operation: Dragoon in the south of France, PFC Phil Kennamer and Lieutenant Harry Moore, of Battery C 460th Parachute Field Artillery Battalion, both armed with submachine guns, surprise-attack a German machine-gun position. Lieutenant Moore fires on the Germans, revealing their position, but Moore's gun jams. Minutes later, both men are found dead. Philip M. Kennamer, the twenty-eight-year-old paratrooper, is face-down with four to five bullet holes across his chest.

The book is now closed on one of the nation's most publicized murders. Phil's premonition that he might not be coming back from war became a reality. Though his life was cut short, Phil got to experience the military life that he'd only read about as a young boy and was able to travel outside the country, which he'd often spoken of doing. If Phil believed in destiny, his fate was now fulfilled. I'm not convinced that Phil had mental issues. He was odd and maybe socially inept, but I believe he was very intelligent and precocious. Phil's predicament was that neither he nor his family knew how to channel that intelligence into something more productive for himself and society.

The following is an eyewitness account of that fateful day:

> After a day or two getting ready, the stage was set. We were to get in the planes at about 100 hours [1 a.m.] on August 15, and get out where they told us.
>
> My outfit was made up mostly of young guys, most of them right out of high school—or in some cases reform school. I was one of the older ones. Phil Kennamer of the Oklahoma State Penitentiary and the pitch games was three or four years older than I was, and partly due to our advanced years we had become pretty good buddies. We couldn't sleep as well as those young kids without nerves, so we sat up and talked till time to load in the planes.
>
> We were out of about everything to talk about, and finally got to religion. He said he didn't believe in God, didn't believe in much of anything. I said, "You mean you think that if you get shot tomorrow it's all over?" He said, "Yep, that's what I think."
>
> We had another lieutenant from a battery, Lt. Roberts, and pretty soon he came with the information that Phil Kennamer and Lt. Moore had just been killed. I got down the line a ways and there they lay. Phil had a nice row of bleeding holes, maybe four or five, across his chest. It had been maybe seven or eight hours since we were talking

about such matters; he then knew more about the hereafter than I did.

Phil had been in the machine gun section with Lark Washburn and a Charlie Nielson from Butte MT. Charley was sort of mourning about old Buffalo Phil. (I'd hung that name on him. He was bad out of shape when he got to our outfit and couldn't keep up on the runs. I said, "Kennamer, you look like a buffalo at the end of a long stampede," and the name stuck. He was an odd character, not your average ex-con. His dad was a federal judge and a figure in Oklahoma politics. Phil was subject to working under Lark Washburn when Lark was a corporal. Phil said to me, "He is a mean man. He worked me like a motherless mule." We still use the term. Oh yes, I ramble.) When Charley Nielson was mourning Phil, Lark said, "Well, it's probably for the best. He was always overbidding his hand."

—"How I Saw It," by Milton D. Rogers,
S/Sgt (ret.) of the 517th Parachute Regimental Combat Team in 2007

PFC Phil Kennamer, taken shortly before his death
(Courtesy of ww2-airborne.us.)

Wednesday, September 27

Franklin E. Kennamer is notified by the War Department that his son Phil was killed in action.

Chapter 9
1945 Onward

- The Wonder Years — What Happened to the Key Players? -

Saturday, October 6, 1945

Charles Coakley, one of Phil's defense attorneys, dies at age sixty-one (*Ada Weekly News*, October 11, 1945, pg. 3). He was widely known for his many prominent federal court cases, including Phil's. In his early career, Coakley shared a law practice with Phil's father, Franklin.

Wednesday, June 9, 1954

Dixie Gilmer, prosecuting attorney, dies in Oklahoma City. He was fifty-three.

Friday, January 31, 1958

Former mayor of Pawnee, Oklahoma, and prosecuting attorney on the Kennamer trial Prentiss Rowe dies. He was seventy-three.

Sunday, May 1, 1960

The white-haired retired federal court judge Franklin E. Kennamer, Phil's father, dies in Chelsea, Oklahoma. He was eighty-one.

Saturday, November 24, 1962

Former Oklahoma attorney general and prosecuting attorney J. Berry King dies at Mercy Hospital in Oklahoma City. He was seventy-four.

June 1972

James A. McCollum, the last attorney of Phil's three-attorney defense team, dies in Pawnee, Oklahoma, at eighty-eight years of age.

Austin Flint Moss, one of the prosecuting attorneys, dies at age seventy-seven.

My Personal Conclusions about the Murder

On that cold, wet Thanksgiving evening, I believe that Sidney Born and Phil arrived early at the hospital, just as John was dropping off his date, right before 11 PM. Eunice testified that John left the driver's side door open, with the gun in that door pocket, while he escorted her to the hospital. Phil recognized John's car and asked Sidney to stop. Phil got out of Sidney's car and, as he approached John's car, saw the gun in the driver's door pocket. Phil took the weapon and climbed in the passenger seat of John's car. Sidney saw what Phil did, then drove away. Phil now had the upper hand when John came back to his car. Phil held the gun on John the entire time while they drove away from the hospital, then shot him in the head at Victor and Forest. About one minute later, Phil fired the second shot into John's head. There was no struggle for the gun, because Phil already had it. The photo that Detective Henry Maddux took showed that John's clothing and his hair were not in disarray. Nor was his body in a position that would suggest a struggle had occurred. I believe that Phil falsely testified that there was a struggle to shore up his motive for self-defense.

As for Sidney's death, Sidney knew that Phil had ambushed and killed John. Sidney, a nervous sort, felt he was also responsible for the murder, because he had driven Phil to the meeting. On that fateful day, Sidney found his father's gun and left the house. Did he take the gun for protection, or was he suffering from a guilty conscience? Was his call to Phil from the drugstore to discuss what had happened to John or to tell Phil "goodbye"? When Sidney's attempt to contact Phil at the jail failed, he grew more despondent, drove to the park, and committed suicide, forever silencing his eyewitness account. I never believed he was murdered. The rumor that a gang had killed Sidney, either for revenge over John's death or for other reasons, came from the fertile minds of young, wealthy teenage boys and was perpetuated by the media.

Acknowledgments

The research and documentation for this book have been a labor of love for many years. I have done my best to make this bit of Tulsa history as accurate as possible. I want to posthumously thank my grandmother, Virginia Wilcox Snedden Hagar, for "tipping" me off about this story by leaving the cardboard box of newspaper clippings about it in her guestroom closet. Grandma, my only regret is that you and I didn't get to talk about it while you were alive. But I understand.

Many thanks to the *Tulsa World* and the *Tulsa Tribune* for their extensive coverage of the trial and the coverage of events before and after it. Thanks also to the great staff whom I got to know at the Tulsa City-County library, while I spent days and many hours pouring over the microfiche of these two newspapers to do the research during my out-of-state visits to Tulsa. I would not have gotten through it without your help. Thank you.

My thanks to author and writer Jason Morrow for sharing with me some of your research and pictures. Coincidentally, Jason and I accidentally met at the library in the microfiche room, while we were both researching material for our books. I enjoyed working with you.

The subscription to Ancestry.com has been very helpful. From its website, I was able to search newspapers for details on many of the cast and characters after the trial, which made me realize just how far reaching the publicity about the trial was across the nation.

To S/Sgt. Milton D. Rogers, thanks for your perspective on Phil Kennamer while you served in the 460th Battery C, 517th parachute regimental combat team. Many details about Phil's early life were brought up during the trial, but your writing allowed us to get a glimpse of Phil as an adult and a soldier. Thank you. And thank you for your service!

Many thanks to my editor, Patricia Waldygo, for taking on my project. Your invaluable suggestions and attention to detail improved the depth and body of this book. You are greatly appreciated.

April 2001
Virginia Wilcox Snedden Hagar, the author, and Virginia's great-granddaughter, Danielle Freese taken outside of Virginia's home

Made in the USA
Middletown, DE
25 October 2017